"Sanctify them in the truth; your word is truth."
John 17:3

YOUR WORD IS TRUTH

Being Sanctified In the Truth

EDWARD D. ANDREWS

YOUR WORD IS TRUTH

Being Sanctified In the Truth

Edward D. Andrews

Christian Publishing House
Cambridge, Ohio

Copyright © 2023 Edward D. Andrews

All rights reserved. Except for brief quotations in articles, other publications, book reviews, and blogs, no part of this book may be reproduced in any manner without prior written permission from the publishers. For information, write, support@christianpublishers.org

Unless otherwise stated, Scripture quotations are from Updated American Standard Version (UASV) Copyright © 2022 by Christian Publishing House

YOUR WORD IS TRUTH: Being Sanctified In the Truth by Edward D. Andrews

ISBN-10: 194575706X

ISBN-13: 978-1945757068

Table of Contents

Book Description 8
Preface 10
Introduction 12

PSALM 15:2 He Speaks Truth In His Heart 14
    The Importance of Inner Truth 14
    The Role of Honesty in Spiritual Growth 16
    Contrast with a Deceptive Heart 18
    Truthfulness as a Pathway to Righteousness 20

PSALM 25:5 Lead Me in Your Truth and Teach Me 24
    The Prayer for Divine Guidance 24
    The Intersection of Truth and Learning 26
    Trusting God's Leadership 28
    Steps to Spiritual Discernment 30

PSALM 26:3 I Will Walk In Your Truth 33
    Commitment to God's Truth 33
    The Pathway of Integrity 35
    God's Truth as Moral Compass 36
    The Link Between Truth and Obedience 38

PROVERBS 23:23 Buy Truth—Do Not Sell It 44
    The Intrinsic Value of Truth 44
    The Cost of Acquiring Wisdom 46
    The Dangers of Trading Truth 48
    The Lasting Investment in Integrity 50

JOHN 4:23 Worship the Father in Spirit and Truth 53
    Defining Authentic Worship 53
    The Role of Spirit in Worship 55
    The Importance of Truth in Worship 57
    The Convergence of Spirit and Truth 59

JOHN 8:32 The Truth Will Set You Free 62
    The Power of Truth 62
    The Chains of Ignorance 64

- Truth as a Path to Freedom 66
- The Liberating Message of Jesus 67

JOHN 17:17 Your Word Is Truth 70
- The Divine Source of Truth 70
- The Role of Scripture in Spiritual Life 72
- Truth as a Means of Sanctification 74
- The Efficacy of God's Word 76

JOHN 18:38 What Is Truth 80
- Pilate's Puzzling Question 80
- The Nature of Biblical Truth 82
- The Relativism of the World 84
- The Answer Found in Christ 86

ROMANS 1:18 Unrighteous Men Who Suppress the Truth 89
- The Act of Suppressing Truth 89
- Consequences of Unrighteousness 91
- The Role of Human Rebellion 93
- Divine Wrath and Truth Suppressed 95

2 CORINTHIANS 4:2 Not Adulterating the Word of God by Making the Truth Manifest 98
- The Integrity of the Gospel Message 98
- The Danger of Distorting God's Word 100
- Manifesting Truth in Ministry 102
- The Accountability of Spiritual Leaders 104

EPHESIANS 1:13 Having Heard the Word of Truth, the Gospel of Your Salvation 107
- The Reception of Divine Truth 107
- The Gospel as the Word of Truth 109
- The Personal Nature of Salvation 111
- The Assurance of Faith 113

2 TIMOTHY 2:15 Rightly Handling the Word of Truth 116
- The Responsibility of Scripture Handling 116
- The Importance of Accurate Interpretation 118
- Skills for Truthful Exegesis 120

Accountability Before God in Teaching 122

HEBREWS 10:26 If We Go on Sinning Deliberately after Receiving the Accurate Knowledge of the Truth 125

The Gravity of Deliberate Sin 125

The Role of Accurate Knowledge 127

The Intersection of Truth and Accountability 129

The Consequences of Ignoring Truth 131

JAMES 5:19 If Any Among You Strays from the Truth and One Turns Him Back 134

The Risk of Straying from Truth 134

The Community's Role in Restoration 136

The Importance of Vigilance 138

The Reward of Reclaiming a Straying Soul 140

1 PETER 1:22 By Your Obedience to the Truth 144

The Call to Obedience 144

Truth as the Foundation for Christian Living 146

The Link Between Obedience and Love 148

The Outcomes of Truthful Obedience 150

1 JOHN 2:21 No Lie Is of the Truth 153

The Incompatibility of Lies and Truth 153

Discerning Spiritual Deception 155

The Importance of Abiding in Truth 157

The Role of Integrity in Faith 159

2 JOHN 1:1-2 All Who Know the Truth Because of the Truth that Remains in Us 162

The Community Bound by Truth 162

The Enduring Nature of Divine Truth 164

The Reciprocal Relationship Between Knowing and Living the Truth 166

The Unified Testimony of Truthful Lives 168

Bibliography 171

Book Description

"Your Word Is Truth: Being Sanctified In the Truth"

In a world filled with moral ambiguity and shifting values, the quest for truth remains paramount. "Your Word Is Truth" is a profound exploration of truth's significance in the life of a believer, drawing from the rich tapestry of the Bible's timeless wisdom.

Discover the Essence of Inner Truth: Unveil the importance of cultivating inner honesty as the foundation of spiritual growth. Explore how living in truthfulness can lead to righteousness and a deeper connection with God.

Navigate Divine Guidance: Journey through Psalms to understand the prayer for divine guidance and the intersection of truth and learning. Learn to trust God's leadership and unlock the steps to spiritual discernment.

Walk the Path of Integrity: Dive into the Book of Proverbs to grasp the intrinsic value of truth and the cost of acquiring wisdom. Beware of the dangers of trading truth, and embrace the lasting investment in integrity.

Worship in Spirit and Truth: Explore authentic worship through the Gospel of John, emphasizing the role of the Spirit in worship and the importance of truth in our praise.

The Liberating Power of Truth: Follow the liberating message of Jesus in John's Gospel, as we delve into the profound statement, "The truth will set you free." Understand the chains of ignorance and how truth serves as the path to spiritual freedom.

Foundations of Divine Truth: Investigate the nature of Biblical truth and the relativism of the world, discovering the ultimate answer found in Christ. Uncover the consequences of unrighteousness and the role of human rebellion in divine wrath.

Integrity in Ministry: Gain insight into the integrity of the Gospel message in 2 Corinthians. Grasp the danger of distorting God's Word and the importance of manifesting truth in ministry.

Scripture Handling and Accountability: In 2 Timothy, explore the responsibility of handling Scripture with care, including the importance of accurate interpretation, skills for truthful exegesis, and accountability before God in teaching.

The Gravity of Deliberate Sin: In Hebrews, understand the gravity of deliberate sin after receiving accurate knowledge of the truth. Explore the intersection of truth and accountability, as well as the consequences of ignoring truth.

Community Restoration: Delve into James to examine the risks of straying from the truth and the crucial role of the community in restoration. Discover the importance of vigilance and the rewarding journey of reclaiming a straying soul.

Obedience to the Truth: In 1 Peter, embrace the call to obedience and recognize truth as the foundation for Christian living. Explore the link between obedience and love, and the outcomes of truthful obedience.

The Battle Against Lies: In 1 John, grasp the incompatibility of lies and truth, and learn to discern spiritual deception. Understand the importance of abiding in truth and the role of integrity in faith.

The Community Bound by Truth: Finally, in 2 John, explore the enduring nature of divine truth and the reciprocal relationship between knowing and living the truth. Discover the power of the unified testimony of truthful lives.

"Your Word Is Truth" is a comprehensive journey through the Bible's teachings on truth, offering profound insights, practical wisdom, and guidance for living a life sanctified in the truth. This book is a valuable resource for believers seeking to align their lives with the eternal and unchanging truth of God's Word.

Preface

In a world where truth seems elusive and ever-shifting, the quest for unwavering, eternal truth remains at the heart of the human spirit. It is a journey that transcends time, culture, and circumstance, reaching deep into the core of our existence. As we embark on this exploration of truth within the pages of "Your Word Is Truth: Being Sanctified In the Truth," we are invited to dive headfirst into the unchanging waters of divine wisdom.

This book seeks to unravel the profound significance of truth in the life of a believer, drawing its inspiration from the timeless teachings of the Bible. We journey through the sacred scriptures, uncovering the layers of truth that have sustained generations of faithful souls. It is our hope that this journey will strengthen your faith, deepen your understanding of God's Word, and equip you with the tools to live a life sanctified in the truth.

Throughout this book, we will explore the multifaceted nature of truth as it intersects with various aspects of our spiritual journey. From the inner chambers of our hearts to the communal bonds of worship and accountability, truth weaves a tapestry that connects us with the divine and with one another.

Each chapter delves into a specific facet of truth, often guided by the profound insights of the Psalms, Proverbs, and the teachings of Jesus and the apostles. We begin with the importance of inner truth, where we learn that honesty and integrity are the building blocks of spiritual growth. We delve into the prayer for divine guidance, recognizing that truth is the compass that directs our steps in a world filled with distractions and detours.

The path of integrity becomes our guiding light, as we understand that God's truth serves as our moral compass, leading us toward righteousness. We explore the depths of worship in spirit and truth, discovering that our praise is most authentic when it aligns with the truth of who God is. We also confront the chains of ignorance and celebrate the liberating message of Jesus, who declared, "The truth will set you free."

The book further delves into the foundations of divine truth, understanding that the Bible provides an unshakable anchor in a relativistic world. We recognize that truth is not merely an abstract concept but a living reality found in the person of Christ.

As we journey through the New Testament, we uncover the responsibility of handling Scripture with care, emphasizing the importance of accurate interpretation and accountability before God in teaching. The gravity of deliberate sin after receiving accurate knowledge of the truth becomes apparent, highlighting the consequences of ignoring truth.

Restoration and vigilance in the faith community are also explored, reminding us that we are called to support one another on our journey of faith. We uncover the link between obedience and love, recognizing that our obedience to the truth is a natural outpouring of love for our Creator.

In the battle against lies and deception, we sharpen our discernment, learning to distinguish between falsehood and divine truth. We understand that truth is not an isolated pursuit but a communal endeavor that binds us together as a community of believers.

The journey culminates in the recognition of the enduring nature of divine truth and the reciprocal relationship between knowing and living the truth. We witness the power of truthful lives as they testify to the transformative power of God's Word.

As we embark on this exploration of truth, may your heart be stirred, your faith deepened, and your life sanctified in the truth of God's Word. Together, let us embark on a journey that transcends time and culture, finding our anchor in the eternal truth that has sustained generations and continues to guide us today.

Edward D. Andrews

Author of 220+ books and the Chief Translator of the Updated American Standard Version

Introduction

In an era defined by shifting sands of opinion, fluctuating moral compasses, and a cacophony of voices vying for our attention, the quest for truth remains a timeless and unwavering pursuit. It is a pursuit that has transcended generations, cultures, and worldviews, seeking to unravel the mysteries of existence, purpose, and meaning. Within the pages of "Your Word Is Truth: Being Sanctified In the Truth," we embark on a journey into the heart of this enduring quest for truth as it is understood through the lens of conservative Christian scholarship.

In a world where truth is often subjective and relative, we turn to the unchanging and eternal truth found within the pages of the Bible. This sacred text has been a source of guidance, comfort, and transformation for countless individuals throughout history. As we delve into the exploration of truth, we do so with the firm belief that the Bible serves as the foundation, compass, and source of truth for the Christian faith.

Our journey through these pages will take us on a multifaceted exploration of truth, drawing inspiration from the Psalms, Proverbs, and the teachings of Jesus and the apostles. It is a journey that touches the deepest recesses of our hearts, challenges our preconceptions, and beckons us to align our lives with divine truth.

At its core, this book is a testament to the enduring relevance and power of God's Word. It serves as a guide for those who seek to navigate the complexities of life with a steadfast commitment to truth. As we delve into the chapters that follow, we will encounter truth in its various dimensions, each shedding light on a unique facet of our spiritual journey.

We begin with the importance of inner truth, recognizing that truthfulness and integrity are the cornerstones of authentic Christian living. Honesty in our hearts becomes the wellspring from which all other aspects of truth flow.

In our quest for truth, we find ourselves uttering the prayer found in Psalm 25:5, "Lead me in your truth and teach me." This heartfelt plea acknowledges our dependence on divine guidance in a world filled with competing voices and worldviews. We recognize that God's truth is not a distant concept but a guiding force that directs our steps.

As we journey deeper, we explore the path of integrity, realizing that God's truth serves as our moral compass, steering us toward righteousness. It is in the alignment of our lives with this divine truth that we find the pathway to genuine righteousness.

Our exploration also takes us into the realm of worship, where we discover that authentic worship is rooted in both spirit and truth. We learn that our praise and adoration of God are most genuine when they align with the truth of who God is.

Yet, our journey is not without its challenges. We confront the chains of ignorance that bind us and celebrate the liberating message of Jesus, who declared, "The truth will set you free." In a world where misinformation and falsehoods abound, we find solace and freedom in the truth of Christ.

As we delve into the New Testament, we uncover the foundations of divine truth, understanding that the Bible itself is an unshakable anchor in a world of shifting sands. We realize that truth is not an abstract concept but a living reality found in the person of Christ.

Our journey also leads us to the responsibility of handling Scripture with care, emphasizing the importance of accurate interpretation and accountability before God in teaching. We are confronted with the gravity of deliberate sin after receiving accurate knowledge of the truth and the sobering consequences of ignoring truth.

In our exploration, we recognize the importance of restoration and vigilance within the faith community, acknowledging that we are called to support one another on our journey of faith. We see the link between obedience and love, understanding that our obedience to the truth is a natural outpouring of love for our Creator.

In the battle against lies and deception, we sharpen our discernment, learning to distinguish between falsehood and divine truth. We understand that truth is not an isolated pursuit but a communal endeavor that binds us together as a community of believers.

The journey culminates in the recognition of the enduring nature of divine truth and the reciprocal relationship between knowing and living the truth. We witness the power of truthful lives as they testify to the transformative power of God's Word.

As we embark on this exploration of truth, may your heart be stirred, your faith deepened, and your life sanctified in the truth of God's Word. Together, let us embark on a journey that transcends time and culture, finding our anchor in the eternal truth that has sustained generations and continues to guide us today.

PSALM 15:2 He Speaks Truth In His Heart

The Importance of Inner Truth

The Psalms, a poetic anthology of prayers, hymns, and laments, offer profound insights into the complexities of the human condition and the nature of God. Psalm 15, a brief but penetrating Psalm, delves into the qualities that characterize the individual who may abide in God's presence. One of the attributes underscored in this Psalm is speaking truth in one's heart, mentioned in verse 2: "He who walks blamelessly and does what is right and speaks truth in his heart."

The Structure and Context

Psalm 15 serves as a "Wisdom Psalm," which is similar in some aspects to the Wisdom literature of the Old Testament like Proverbs and Ecclesiastes. It consists of a question-and-answer format; the question posed in verse 1 receives its answer in the subsequent verses. The inquiry is about who may dwell in God's sanctuary, implying a broader question of who may enjoy a close relationship with Jehovah. Among the qualifications listed is the matter of inner truth—truth in the heart.

The Heart as the Seat of Character

Biblically, the "heart" symbolizes the core of a person—the center of thought, emotion, and will. Therefore, to "speak truth in his heart" means to possess integrity that permeates the entire being. This is not merely a superficial truth-telling but a deep-seated commitment to truthfulness that starts from the inside out. It is a truth that is internalized, and not merely performed for outward appearance.

The Concept of Truth in the Bible

Truth, or "emet" in Hebrew, encompasses more than factual accuracy; it involves reliability, faithfulness, and a steadfast adherence to righteousness. The Bible portrays God as the embodiment of truth, making it imperative for those who wish to fellowship with Him to also be committed to truthfulness (John 14:6; Psalm 31:5).

Inner Truth vs. Outward Show

The Pharisees provide a cautionary tale about missing the heart of the matter. Despite their strict adherence to the Law, their righteousness was often an external performance (Matthew 23:27-28). Jesus Christ condemned this as hypocrisy, indicating that God is not merely concerned with outward compliance to rules but is deeply interested in the condition of the heart (Matthew 5:21-22, 27-28).

The Moral Ramifications of Inner Truth

Truth in the heart affects not just our relationship with God but also with fellow humans. Deception and falsehood sow discord and erode trust, dismantling the fabric of community and family (Ephesians 4:25; Colossians 3:9). On the contrary, a heart committed to truth fosters relationships and creates an environment where righteousness can flourish.

The Role of God's Word

One of the essential means by which a believer cultivates truth in the heart is through the Word of God. The Scriptures serve as a mirror that reflects the condition of our inner being (James 1:23-25), and they provide the moral and ethical standards by which we align our hearts and lives (Psalm 119:11). The Apostle Paul reminds us that the Scriptures are beneficial for teaching, reproof, correction, and training in righteousness (2 Timothy 3:16).

Practicable Steps

1. **Self-examination**: Regularly take time to evaluate the sincerity and integrity of your heart (2 Corinthians 13:5).
2. **Confession and Repentance**: Acknowledge and turn away from dishonesty and deceit (1 John 1:9).
3. **Word Saturation**: Fill your mind and heart with God's Word through study and meditation (Psalm 1:2).
4. **Prayer**: Constantly seek God's help to maintain a heart that is pure and truthful (Psalm 51:10).
5. **Accountability**: Maintain relationships with godly individuals who can provide corrective measures and encouragement (Proverbs 27:17).

Living in Alignment with God's Character

Truth is not just something God values; it's an essential aspect of His character. The call to speak truth in one's heart is not a mere moral injunction; it's a call to align ourselves with the very nature of God. As we internalize truth, we reflect God's image more accurately, fulfilling our ultimate purpose of glorifying Him and enjoying fellowship with Him.

While it is challenging to maintain inner truth in a world that often rewards deceit and superficiality, the promise of dwelling in the presence of Jehovah offers a compelling motivation. For the individual committed to inner truth, the prospect is not merely earthly benefits but eternal communion with God, a reality that far outweighs the challenges of practicing truth in a fallen world. Amen.

The Role of Honesty in Spiritual Growth

The concept of honesty holds an indispensable place in the Christian walk. It serves as one of the foundational pillars supporting spiritual growth and maturity. Although the Bible mentions honesty in various contexts, it often does so with the intent of directing believers toward a deeper, more authentic relationship with Jehovah. This essay aims to unpack the multifaceted role of honesty in spiritual growth.

Honesty with God

The foremost aspect of spiritual honesty begins with our relationship with Jehovah. David, the psalmist, provides a profound example in his heartfelt confessions, as seen in Psalm 51. He does not merely acknowledge his sin; he also expresses the deep remorse that permeates his heart. This level of transparency is crucial for growth, as it invites Jehovah's cleansing and renewal. God's desire is for "truth in the inward being" (Psalm 51:6 ESV).

Honesty with Ourselves

The second aspect of spiritual honesty involves being truthful with ourselves. Self-deception can be an insidious obstacle to growth. The Apostle Paul emphasizes self-examination when he says, "Examine yourselves, to see whether you are in the faith. Test yourselves" (2 Corinthians 13:5 ESV). Introspection guided by the Holy Scriptures is not a narcissistic activity but a necessity for anyone intent on spiritual growth.

Honesty in Interpersonal Relationships

Honesty extends its influence into our relationships with others. The Apostle Paul instructs the Ephesian church to "put away falsehood" and to "speak the truth with his neighbor" (Ephesians 4:25 ESV). Honesty in relationships promotes trust and fosters an environment where spiritual growth can thrive. In a dishonest environment, on the other hand, true growth is hindered, and the emotional and spiritual health of the community suffers.

Honesty and Repentance

True honesty leads to repentance, which is a pivotal component of spiritual growth. Without repentance, we become stagnant in our Christian life. The story of the prodigal son in Luke 15 is a striking illustration of how honesty precedes repentance. When the son "came to himself," acknowledging his wretched state, it propelled him back to his father. The act of returning was initiated by an honest assessment of his life.

Honesty as a Protection Against Sin

The essence of honesty can act as a shield against sin. When we are truly honest, the temptation to sin is met with the full weight of truth, which often exposes the folly of the sinful path. Honesty acts as a gatekeeper, aligning our hearts and minds with God's standards, thus enabling us to make choices that lead to spiritual growth.

Honesty and Prayer

The discipline of prayer becomes significantly more effective when exercised in honesty. A prayer life lacking honesty becomes ritualistic and shallow. James 5:16 tells us to "confess your sins to one another and pray for one another, that you may be healed" (ESV). Here, honesty serves as a catalyst for deeper spiritual interactions, both with God and fellow believers.

Honesty in the Face of Suffering

While God did not design suffering for character development, He allows it to demonstrate the inherent flaw in human independence from His sovereignty. During these trials, honesty continues to play a pivotal role. An honest acknowledgment of our frailty in the face of suffering can lead us to a deeper reliance on God, thus contributing to our spiritual growth.

In summary, honesty serves as a multifaceted tool in the journey of spiritual growth. It fosters a deeper relationship with Jehovah, encourages self-examination, enriches interpersonal relationships, leads to genuine repentance, acts as a protective shield against sin, and deepens our prayer life. The Christian who neglects honesty risks stagnation and spiritual decline, while those who embrace it find themselves on a fruitful path toward spiritual maturity and a deeper relationship with Jehovah. Therefore, let us strive to be individuals who "speak truth in [our] heart" (Psalm 15:2 ESV), fully recognizing the invaluable role of honesty in our spiritual growth.

Contrast with a Deceptive Heart

The essence of a believer's relationship with Jehovah is deeply intertwined with the condition of the heart. Psalm 15:2, highlighting a key aspect of godly living, states, "He who walks blamelessly and does what is right and speaks truth in his heart" (ESV). In contrast, Jeremiah 17:9 warns that "the heart is deceitful above all things, and desperately sick; who can understand it?" (ESV). These two Scriptural references set the stage for understanding the stark contrast between a heart that speaks truth and one that is deceptive.

Speaking Truth in One's Heart: A Foundation for Godliness

The individual who "speaks truth in his heart" is not merely one who refrains from lying but is someone whose innermost being aligns with Jehovah's truth. This alignment serves as the backbone for ethical decisions, moral clarity, and a life of integrity. David exemplifies this in his psalms, revealing an inner longing for truth and righteousness, as in Psalm 51:6 where he says, "Behold, you delight in truth in the inward being" (ESV).

Such a heart is a fertile ground for virtues like love, peace, patience, and all the fruit of the Spirit listed in Galatians 5:22-23. It's also a heart well-equipped for the spiritual warfare described in Ephesians 6, particularly for wielding the "sword of the Spirit, which is the word of God" (Ephesians 6:17 ESV).

Deceptive Heart: A Breeding Ground for Sin

In stark contrast, a deceptive heart is marked by duplicity, manipulation, and falsehood. Such a heart can justify sin, minimize the importance of moral imperatives, and ultimately lead a person away from Jehovah. It's a heart that Solomon warns against in Proverbs 4:23, "Keep your heart with all vigilance, for from it flow the springs of life" (ESV).

A deceptive heart often leads to a life characterized by sin and its consequences. Sin not only separates one from Jehovah but also disrupts community life, affects personal growth, and can even lead to various forms of destruction. Indeed, the individual with a deceptive heart may not even recognize his need for Jehovah's grace or the redemptive work of Jesus Christ.

Impact on Relationships: Community and Fellowship

A heart that speaks truth fosters healthy relationships. Honesty serves as a bridge that facilitates genuine fellowship among believers, as seen in Acts 2:42-47, where the early Christians thrived in a community defined by godly sincerity and openness.

On the other hand, a deceptive heart erodes trust and undermines relationships. A person with a deceptive heart can be likened to Ananias and Sapphira (Acts 5), whose deceit not only cost them their lives but also served as a cautionary tale for the entire Christian community.

Impact on Spiritual Growth

Speaking truth in one's heart fosters spiritual growth by aligning one's will with Jehovah's will. This alignment brings blessings and maturity as promised in Joshua 1:8, "This Book of the Law shall not depart from your mouth, but you shall meditate on it day and night, so that you may be careful to do according to all that is written in it. For then you will make your way prosperous, and then you will have good success" (ESV).

A deceptive heart, however, stifles spiritual growth. It leads to a form of godliness but denies its power (2 Timothy 3:5), effectively halting any real progress in spiritual maturity. It keeps individuals in a perpetual state of spiritual infancy, vulnerable to every form of doctrinal error and moral failure.

Confronting Suffering

During times of suffering, the difference between these two types of hearts becomes even more apparent. A heart that speaks truth can lead one into a deeper reliance on Jehovah. It can serve to deepen faith even when circumstances are daunting, allowing the individual to say, like Job, "Though he slay me, I will hope in him" (Job 13:15 ESV). Although God did not design suffering for character development, a truthful heart leads to trust in Jehovah's sovereignty in the midst of suffering.

Conversely, a deceptive heart can lead to bitterness, anger, and a turning away from Jehovah. When faced with trials, instead of drawing near to God, the deceptive heart often leads individuals into further deception, questioning God's goodness and distancing themselves from the source of all comfort and peace.

The contrast between a heart that speaks truth and a deceptive heart is stark and has profound implications for every facet of Christian life. The heart that speaks truth fosters a life of godliness, healthy relationships, robust spiritual growth, and resilience during suffering. In contrast, a deceptive heart leads to a life characterized by sin, broken relationships, stagnant spiritual growth, and a turning away from Jehovah especially in times of difficulty. Thus, a deliberate cultivation of a heart that speaks truth is not just commendable; it is essential for anyone seeking to live in accordance with Jehovah's divine plan.

Truthfulness as a Pathway to Righteousness

The concept of truth is foundational to the Christian faith. It is not merely a moral attribute but is woven into the very fabric of godly living. Jesus declares Himself as "the way, and the truth, and the life" (John 14:6 ESV), emphasizing the inextricable link between truth and righteousness. While our righteousness is ultimately established through faith in Jesus Christ and His finished work on the Cross, living in truth serves as a pathway that leads us toward a righteous life. This essay will explore how truthfulness shapes our character, impacts our relationship with Jehovah, and influences our witness to the world.

Truth in the Context of Scripture

The Hebrew and Greek words for truth ('emet' in Hebrew and 'aletheia' in Greek) occur hundreds of times in the Scriptures. They refer not just to factual accuracy but to reliability, faithfulness, and integrity. In the Old Testament, Jehovah is often described as a "God of truth" (Deuteronomy 32:4 ESV), and His word is the "word of truth" (Psalm 119:43 ESV). The New Testament writers, too, emphasize the importance of truth in the life of a believer, exhorting Christians to "speak the truth in love" (Ephesians 4:15 ESV) and to "walk in the truth" (3 John 1:4 ESV).

Truthfulness as an Attribute of God

Jehovah is the ultimate embodiment of truth. His nature is described in terms like "faithful and true" (Revelation 19:11 ESV), and His Word is described as "living and active" (Hebrews 4:12 ESV). When we align our lives with the truth, we essentially align ourselves with Jehovah's character. This alignment is not a mere moral exercise but an ontological necessity for the believer. It is an essential part of our sanctification and growth in righteousness.

The Individual Aspect: Inner Transformation

When truthfulness is internalized, it transforms the heart, the control center of human emotion, will, and intellect. This inner transformation manifests itself in a life that reflects the righteousness of God. The Apostle Paul encourages believers to "put on the new self, created after the likeness of God in true righteousness and holiness" (Ephesians 4:24 ESV).

The person who values truth will shun deceit, hypocrisy, and dishonesty, embracing instead integrity, transparency, and authenticity. This individual would heed the words of Psalm 15:2, which speaks of the one who "walks blamelessly and does what is right and speaks truth in his heart" (ESV).

The Community Aspect: Building Trust and Fostering Relationships

Truthfulness is not just a personal virtue but a communal asset. A community where truth is held in high regard is one where relationships are deep, meaningful, and reflective of God's kingdom. In such a setting, trust flourishes and facilitates other virtues like love, patience, and humility. The Apostle John commends Gaius, saying, "I have no greater joy than to hear that my children are walking in the truth" (3 John 1:4 ESV). Truthfulness contributes to a community that reflects the righteousness of Jehovah, thereby fulfilling His intentions for His people.

Truthfulness in Witness and Evangelism

Our commitment to truth is also a measure of our credibility as witnesses for Christ. When truth is compromised, so is our witness. In an era marked by relativism and skepticism, a life marked by truthfulness serves as a compelling testimony to the transformative power of the Gospel. Truthfulness, combined with love and humility, can break through even the hardest of hearts.

Practical Implications: Righteousness in Times of Suffering

Truthfulness also serves as a bulwark in times of suffering and trials. A life committed to truth is better equipped to understand and accept the harsh realities that accompany human existence in a fallen world. While God did not design suffering for character development, recognizing the sovereignty of Jehovah in times of suffering can strengthen our resolve and deepen our faith. Truthfulness equips us to deal with suffering in a manner that brings glory to Jehovah and attests to our hope in eternal life.

Truthfulness is a vital character quality that significantly influences our spiritual condition and relationship with Jehovah. Scripture is replete with calls for honesty, integrity, and truthfulness as prerequisites for a life that is pleasing to God. One might look at Ephesians 4:25 as a foundational text in this regard: "Therefore, having put away falsehood, let each one of you speak the truth with his neighbor, for we are members one of another" (ESV). This essay will explore the role of truthfulness as a pathway to righteousness, grounded in a clear understanding of Biblical teachings.

Truthfulness in the Old Testament

From the very beginnings of Hebrew Scripture, truthfulness is extolled as a divine attribute and human obligation. The Ten Commandments include the edict, "You shall not bear false witness against your neighbor" (Exodus 20:16 ESV). In Psalm 15, the psalmist lays down the characteristics of the one who may dwell in Jehovah's holy hill, stating that it's the person who "speaks truth in his heart" (Psalm 15:2 ESV).

In the Old Testament, truthfulness is not just an ethical command; it's part of the character of Jehovah Himself. As Psalm 31:5 states, "Into your hand I commit my spirit; you have redeemed me, O Jehovah, faithful God" (ESV). The faithfulness or truthfulness of Jehovah is the standard by which all human truthfulness is to be measured.

Truthfulness in the New Testament

The New Testament continues this emphasis on truthfulness as crucial for righteousness. In his epistle to the Colossians, Paul urges, "Do not lie to one another, seeing that you have put off the old self with its practices and have put on the new self, which is being renewed in knowledge after the image of its creator" (Colossians 3:9-10 ESV). Paul links lying with the old self and truthfulness with the new self, which is modeled after the image of God.

Jesus, too, equated truthfulness with godliness. In His high priestly prayer recorded in John 17, He prays, "Sanctify them in the truth; your word is truth" (John 17:17 ESV). Jesus points to God's word as the ultimate standard of truth that sanctifies, or makes believers holy.

Truthfulness and the Church

The early Christian community saw truthfulness as essential for communal health and integrity. Acts 5 recounts the story of Ananias and Sapphira, who were struck dead for lying to the apostles and, by extension, to God. Their deceit fractured the integrity of the community and warranted swift judgment.

Truthfulness within the body of Christ serves to build trust, promote transparency, and enhance Christian fellowship. The early church's communal life as depicted in Acts 2:42-47 was likely made possible because of a commitment to truthfulness among its members.

Truthfulness and Personal Righteousness

On an individual level, truthfulness is essential for spiritual growth and maturity. It enables a person to honestly examine himself, recognize sin, and confess it before Jehovah. First John 1:9 asserts, "If we confess our sins, he is faithful and just to forgive us our sins and to cleanse us from all unrighteousness" (ESV). An honest heart is necessary for this confession and subsequent forgiveness.

Truthfulness aligns our innermost thoughts with Jehovah's will, leading to a life characterized by godly wisdom, as in James 3:17, which states that "the wisdom from above is first pure, then peaceable, gentle, open to reason, full of mercy and good fruits, impartial and sincere" (ESV).

In sum, truthfulness is not just an ethical choice but a pathway to righteousness. It transforms the individual, enriches the community, and strengthens the witness of the Church. It prepares us for life's trials and fortifies our faith in Jehovah's ultimate purpose for humanity. As we continually seek to be molded in the image of Christ, let us strive for truthfulness in every aspect of our lives, so that we may "be filled with all the fullness of God" (Ephesians 3:19 ESV) and walk in the righteousness that He desires for us.

PSALM 25:5 Lead Me in Your Truth and Teach Me

The Prayer for Divine Guidance

One of the themes that reverberate through the Psalms is the plea for guidance from Jehovah. Psalm 25:5 states, "Lead me in your truth and teach me, for you are the God of my salvation; for you I wait all the day long" (ESV). This prayer encapsulates the profound relationship between divine guidance, the pursuit of truth, and the believer's posture of humble waiting. As a conservative Bible scholar, this essay will unpack the Psalmist's plea in Psalm 25:5, demonstrating how it serves as an example and a guide for those seeking Jehovah's direction in their lives.

The Context of Psalm 25

Psalm 25 is generally considered to be a Psalm of David, reflecting his dependence on Jehovah, especially in times of distress. He employs acrostic forms, possibly as a mnemonic device or as a poetic way to convey that he is discussing comprehensive topics that affect the entirety of life. In the Psalm, David recognizes his sinfulness and pleads for forgiveness, guidance, and deliverance. He does not just want to avoid adversity; he desires to understand and walk in Jehovah's ways.

The Components of the Prayer

Let's dissect Psalm 25:5 into its constituent parts for a deeper understanding:

1. **"Lead me in your truth"**: The Psalmist requests active guidance from Jehovah. This is not a passive receiving of information but a daily, moment-to-moment leading. The Hebrew word for "lead" denotes to guide or to conduct and is often used in the context of shepherding. The term "truth" refers to Jehovah's divine reality, immutable and everlasting.

2. **"And teach me"**: Teaching is an active process involving both the teacher and the student. Here, the Psalmist acknowledges that he has much to learn. It is the continuous revelation of Jehovah's statutes, commandments, and decrees that the Psalmist seeks.

3. **"For you are the God of my salvation"**: This acknowledges that salvation is not just an event but a process. While physical deliverance is essential, the Psalmist has a broader view of salvation that includes living in alignment with Jehovah's truth.

4. **"For you I wait all the day long"**: Waiting is an active form of trust. The Psalmist acknowledges that divine guidance doesn't usually come instantly but through a process of active waiting that involves listening, obeying, and trusting.

The Interplay of Truth and Teaching

There is an implicit recognition that divine truth is not merely cognitive but deeply experiential. It is not enough to have a theoretical grasp of truth; it must be walked out daily. Jehovah's "teaching" therefore includes not only revealing the truth but providing opportunities for its practical application. The Hebrew word for "teach," 'lamad,' signifies a form of learning that involves habit or action.

The Role of the Believer: Active Waiting

The believer's role in this divine-human relationship is not passive. The Psalmist is committed to "wait all the day long." This implies patience, trust, and vigilance. Waiting for Jehovah is not a mere pause but a committed expectation that God will come through, akin to a watchman who waits for the morning light.

Practical Application for Modern Believers

Modern-day believers can find in Psalm 25:5 a model prayer when seeking guidance in important decisions, whether they be ethical dilemmas, life changes, or any other significant issues.

1. **Pray for Jehovah's leading:** Openly ask for God's guidance and be willing to follow it when it comes.
2. **Study the Scriptures:** The Bible is the revealed Word of God and provides principles for life and godliness. Therefore, understanding God's truth often begins by immersing oneself in Scripture.
3. **Active Waiting:** Sometimes Jehovah's guidance doesn't come immediately. In such cases, waiting actively and patiently for His direction is required.

Psalm 25:5 is a powerful prayer for those seeking Jehovah's guidance. The Psalmist does not merely ask for a one-time direction but a continuous leading in the paths of divine truth. This request includes both a willingness to be taught and a humble disposition to wait upon Jehovah. For the modern believer, this prayer serves as a critical reminder that the pursuit of divine guidance is not a momentary quest but a lifetime endeavor.

By internalizing this prayer's components and principles, one can deepen their walk with Jehovah, rooted in the truth of His word and open to the ongoing work of His guiding hand.

The Intersection of Truth and Learning

The pursuit of truth and the enterprise of learning are not isolated endeavors but intricately connected aspects of the Christian journey. Both the Old and New Testaments shed light on the role of truth and learning as avenues to a deeper relationship with Jehovah. As a conservative Bible scholar, I aim to explore this symbiotic relationship by examining key Scriptural passages and principles, thereby establishing that a commitment to truth is indispensable to authentic Christian learning, and vice versa.

Defining Terms: What is Truth? What is Learning?

In a Scriptural context, "truth" goes beyond mere factual accuracy. It encapsulates moral integrity, the nature of Jehovah, and the foundational principles that govern life. The Hebrew term often translated as "truth" is 'emet,' which signifies firmness, reliability, and stability. The Greek equivalent is 'aletheia,' used in the New Testament to denote the reality lying at the basis of an appearance.

"Learning," on the other hand, entails a process of acquiring understanding or skill. The Hebrew term 'lamad' denotes not just the intake of information but a form of learning that influences one's behavior. In the New Testament, terms like 'manthanó' point to understanding derived from experience or practice.

A Strong Biblical Tradition of Learning

From the days of the patriarchs, learning has been a cornerstone of faith. Abraham learned to trust Jehovah through a series of trials and revelations. The Israelites were instructed to teach their children the Law, ensuring that learning was intergenerational (Deuteronomy 6:6-7). The wisdom literature, such as the book of Proverbs, is an educational treatise. Proverbs 1:7 famously states, "The fear of the Lord is the beginning of knowledge; fools despise wisdom and instruction" (ESV). Here, the foundation of all learning is an awe-filled recognition of Jehovah's authority.

The Inseparability of Truth and Learning

A common thread that runs through Biblical instruction is that true learning cannot occur apart from the truth. Consider the Apostle Paul, who before his conversion was a learned man, yet he described his previous learning as "rubbish" compared to the knowledge of Christ (Philippians 3:8).

1. **Truth is the Foundation of Learning**: Without a commitment to truth, learning becomes aimless and potentially misleading. Truth anchors learning, giving it purpose and direction. In the words of Jesus, "If you abide in my word, you are truly my disciples, and you will know the truth, and the truth will set you free" (John 8:31-32, ESV).

2. **Learning Leads to a Deeper Understanding of Truth**: Conversely, a pursuit of truth necessitates constant learning. Truth is not static; our understanding deepens over time through study, prayer, and experience.

3. **Truth Transforms**: Romans 12:2 emphasizes the transformative power of renewing our minds, thereby discerning the will of God. Learning that is rooted in truth has the power to change not just the mind but also the heart and actions.

The Role of the Holy Scriptures

The Scriptures serve as the ultimate standard of truth for the believer (2 Timothy 3:16). They are the basis upon which all other learning can be evaluated and are the primary means by which one gains spiritual understanding. The Bible is not just a source of theological facts but a guide for practical living, thereby merging truth and learning in an everyday context.

The Community Aspect: The Intersection in Practice

Christian learning and truth-seeking are not just individual endeavors but also communal activities. The New Testament Church exemplifies this as believers met regularly for teaching and mutual edification (Acts 2:42). The communal dimension adds accountability and a variety of perspectives, enriching both the pursuit of truth and the learning process.

In summary, the Biblical worldview offers a compelling vision of the interplay between truth and learning. Both elements are foundational to spiritual growth and are intrinsically connected. A Christian commitment to truth provides the framework within which genuine learning occurs, while a dedication to learning deepens one's understanding and application of Biblical truth.

The Scriptures serve as the anchor point in this synergistic relationship, guiding believers toward a life that glorifies Jehovah. Whether individually or within the community, the intersection of truth and learning remains a dynamic space where faith is deepened, character is formed, and a closer walk with Jehovah is cultivated. Therefore, any dichotomy between truth and learning is not only artificial but also antithetical to the unified, holistic life that Scripture advocates.

Trusting God's Leadership

Trust in divine leadership is a cornerstone of Biblical faith, touching every aspect of a believer's relationship with Jehovah. From the earliest moments of Scriptural history to the New Testament writings, we see the thread of trust weaving the tapestry of human-divine interactions. This essay aims to explore the concept of trusting God's leadership by examining key Biblical passages and principles, considering the relevance of this trust in the Christian life, and its implications for spiritual growth.

Foundational Definitions

The Hebrew word often translated as "trust" is 'batach,' indicating a secure confidence. The New Testament Greek term 'pisteuo' is closely linked to faith, denoting firm conviction. Leadership, in a divine context, refers to Jehovah's guidance, governance, and providential control over His creation.

Trust in the Old Testament

1. **Abraham:** The patriarch Abraham epitomizes trust in Jehovah's leadership. Called to leave his homeland without knowing his destination, Abraham obeyed (Hebrews 11:8). His trust was not in the clarity of the plan but in the One who planned.
2. **Moses and the Israelites:** In the Exodus narrative, Moses had to trust Jehovah at every turn, be it at the burning bush or at the Red Sea. The Israelites, however, wavered in their trust, and this lack of trust led to a prolonged journey in the wilderness.
3. **King David:** The Psalms, many penned by David, are replete with expressions of trust in Jehovah's leadership, even in times of personal and national crisis. Psalm 23 poetically encapsulates the essence of divine leadership and the resulting peace that comes from trust.

Trust in the New Testament

1. **Jesus Christ:** The ultimate exemplar of trust in divine leadership is Jesus Himself. Whether in the wilderness being tempted, in Gethsemane praying, or on the cross dying—His trust in Jehovah's plan was unwavering.
2. **The Early Church:** Acts and the Epistles show the early Christians navigating persecution, internal conflicts, and missionary endeavors. Their trust in Jehovah's leadership shaped the spread of the Gospel.

The Nature of God's Leadership

1. **Sovereign:** Jehovah is in complete control, orchestrating the events of history toward His intended ends (Romans 8:28).
2. **Personal:** Jehovah's leadership is not distant; it is intimate and involved (Matthew 10:29-31).
3. **Moral:** God's governance is not arbitrary but founded on His holiness and justice (Psalm 89:14).

Obstacles to Trusting God's Leadership

1. **Human Independence:** Trust in Jehovah requires acknowledging our limitations and weaknesses, something that human pride resists.
2. **Fear and Uncertainty:** Fear of the unknown can often overshadow the trustworthiness of the Known—Jehovah.
3. **Misunderstanding of Suffering:** Suffering can often be mistaken as the absence of divine leadership. However, Jehovah allows suffering to demonstrate the inherent flaw in human independence from His sovereignty, as an object lesson for humanity.

The Benefits of Trust

1. **Peace:** Trust in Jehovah's leadership yields an incomparable inner peace (Philippians 4:7).
2. **Wisdom:** Proverbs 3:5-6 promises that trust in Jehovah leads to divine direction.
3. **Spiritual Maturity:** A life led by Jehovah is one of spiritual growth and sanctification (2 Peter 1:3-8).

The Bible presents a compelling case for trusting Jehovah's leadership. It is a trust founded not on transient circumstances but on the unchanging nature of God. By placing our trust in Him, we are not forgoing reason or responsibility; rather, we are recognizing the limitations of human wisdom and capability.

Trusting God's leadership is neither passive resignation nor naïve optimism. It is an active, informed, and intimate relationship with the Creator of the universe, acknowledging His sovereignty over all aspects of life. This trust is not an optional aspect of the Christian experience but a fundamental one. It enriches our understanding of God, shapes our behavior, and fortifies our resilience in times of trials and tribulations. Indeed, trust in Jehovah's leadership is the bedrock upon which a fulfilling and fruitful Christian life is built.

Steps to Spiritual Discernment

Spiritual discernment, the ability to judge well within the context of one's faith, is an indispensable skill for believers striving to walk in accordance with Jehovah's will. This faculty is not innate but cultivated through a dedicated application of Scriptural principles. This essay seeks to elucidate these principles by providing a step-by-step guide to spiritual discernment, grounded in a conservative interpretation of Scripture.

Foundational Definitions

Spiritual discernment is the practiced ability to distinguish between divine truth and human or demonic error. The Greek word for discernment is 'diakrisis,' often associated with discriminating, judging, or distinguishing. The practice of discernment is commended in Hebrews 5:14, indicating it's not just a spiritual gift but a developed skill.

Step 1: Commit to Jehovah and His Word

The foundational step in spiritual discernment is commitment to Jehovah as the ultimate authority and to His Word as the supreme source of wisdom. A firm conviction in 2 Timothy 3:16-17 that "All Scripture is breathed out by God and profitable for teaching, for reproof, for correction, and for training in righteousness," establishes the basis for all subsequent steps.

Step 2: Pray for Wisdom

James 1:5 asserts that if anyone lacks wisdom, they should ask God, who gives generously to all. Prayer serves as a channel for divine wisdom, invoking the Holy Spirit's guidance through the inspired Word of God. Remember, while there is no indwelling of the Holy Spirit, we are guided by the Spirit-inspired Word.

Step 3: Study the Scriptures

Acts 17:11 commends the Bereans for studying the Scriptures to discern the veracity of Paul's teachings. A rigorous study of the Bible in its context helps develop an objective, historical-grammatical understanding that is necessary for discernment.

Step 4: Consult Reliable Biblical Interpretations

While personal study is crucial, believers benefit from the insights of established Biblical scholars who have devoted their lives to understanding the Word. Ensure these scholars align with your conservative, literal approach to Scripture.

Step 5: Be Attentive to Context

Ignoring the context—whether historical, cultural, or grammatical—can lead to eisegesis, or reading one's own interpretation into the text, rather than exegesis, which is drawing out the author's intended meaning.

Step 6: Consider the Fruit

Matthew 7:16-20 tells us that a good tree produces good fruit, and a bad tree produces bad fruit. Assess the outcomes or implications of the interpretation or decision being considered. Are they consistent with Scriptural teachings?

Step 7: Exercise Caution with Extra-Biblical Sources

While other literature can offer valuable insights, they should never supersede the authority of Scripture. 1 Thessalonians 5:21 advises us to "test everything; hold fast what is good."

Step 8: Seek Godly Counsel

Proverbs 11:14 highlights the importance of counsel in making decisions. However, ensure that the counsel aligns with Scriptural principles.

Step 9: Continuously Reevaluate

Discernment is not a one-time event but a continuous process. In light of new information or growth in understanding, be willing to reassess and recalibrate your positions (Proverbs 18:15).

Step 10: Be Prepared to Act

Finally, James 1:22 exhorts us to be "doers of the word, and not hearers only." Discernment that does not lead to action is incomplete and ineffectual.

Spiritual discernment is an integral part of the Christian walk, enabling believers to navigate complex ethical and doctrinal landscapes. Jehovah has given us His Word, the ultimate standard of truth, as well as a community of believers to support us in this endeavor. These steps to spiritual discernment are not a rigid formula but guidelines grounded in a high view of Scripture. By following them, we not only grow in wisdom and maturity but also draw nearer to Jehovah, the source of all truth and wisdom. The goal is not just correct belief or practice but a life transformed to the likeness of Christ, committed to the glory of Jehovah.

Edward D. Andrews

PSALM 26:3 I Will Walk In Your Truth

Commitment to God's Truth

The Psalmist's declaration in Psalm 26:3, "For your steadfast love is before my eyes, and I walk in your faithfulness," provides a critical insight into the essence of living a godly life. This essay aims to explore the idea of commitment to God's truth as expressed in this verse, while appreciating the broader context of Psalm 26. This subject matter is critical for anyone desiring to cultivate spiritual integrity and to gain a deeper understanding of what it means to be committed to God's truth.

The Importance of Commitment to Truth

Before delving into the specifics of Psalm 26:3, it's essential to comprehend why commitment to God's truth is pivotal. Truth serves as the foundation upon which a believer's life should be built. In the Biblical sense, truth is not just propositional but existential. It is not merely to be understood but to be lived out. As the Apostle Paul states in Ephesians 6:14, truth is the belt that holds everything together in the life of a Christian.

Contextual Examination of Psalm 26

To understand verse 3 thoroughly, a brief examination of the Psalm's general context is necessary. David, the presumed author, is making a plea to Jehovah for vindication against false charges. He does so by highlighting his integrity and commitment to God's laws. His claim to "walk in your truth" is not a boast but an acknowledgment of a life dedicated to God's ways.

The Two Pillars: Steadfast Love and Faithfulness

In verse 3, the two key phrases are "your steadfast love is before my eyes," and "I walk in your faithfulness." These represent the pillars upon which David's commitment to truth rests. "Steadfast love" and "faithfulness" are often coupled in the Old Testament to describe God's character. By saying these are "before my eyes," David reveals that his commitment to God's truth is not an abstract notion but something tangible that guides his life daily.

Truth as a Pathway

The metaphor of "walking" in truth indicates an ongoing, active commitment. In Scripture, walking often signifies a way of life (e.g., Ephesians 4:1, 1 John 1:6-7). For David, commitment to God's truth was not limited to rituals or confined to the Temple; it was a lifestyle. It was a pathway marked by ethical conduct, integrity, and most importantly, a deep-seated reverence for Jehovah and His statutes.

Link to New Testament Concepts

It's worth noting that the commitment to walking in God's truth is a recurring theme in the New Testament as well. John, in his second epistle, commends the recipients for "walking in truth," as commanded by the Father (2 John 1:4). Moreover, Jesus himself claimed to be "the way, and the truth, and the life" in John 14:6, reinforcing the idea that commitment to truth is synonymous with a commitment to Christ.

Practical Implications

1. **Regular Scripture Reading and Study**: This is essential for understanding God's truth. A conservative, historical-grammatical method ensures that the text is understood in its original context.
2. **Prayer**: Just like David's relationship with Jehovah, one must continuously seek God's wisdom in prayer (James 1:5).
3. **Ethical Conduct**: Truth is not merely theoretical but practical. It impacts how we interact with others, conduct business, and even how we treat ourselves (Ephesians 4:25, Colossians 3:9).
4. **Community**: Involvement in a community of like-minded believers can provide accountability and encouragement (Hebrews 10:24-25).
5. **Seek Godly Counsel**: The wisdom of mature Christians can offer added perspective and help foster a deeper understanding of God's truth (Proverbs 11:14).

In Psalm 26:3, the psalmist lays down a marker for all those wishing to cultivate a life committed to Jehovah's truth. It serves as a reminder that true spirituality is not merely about rituals or theoretical knowledge but involves a daily, practical commitment to live by God's eternal truth.

This commitment requires a dedication to understanding the Scriptures, ethical living, a lifestyle of prayer, and a willingness to engage in a community of believers for mutual edification. When one chooses to "walk" in Jehovah's truth, he aligns himself with the very character of God—steadfast love and faithfulness—and creates a life not merely of religious observation but of profound spiritual integrity.

The Pathway of Integrity

Integrity is a term often used but seldom explored in depth from a Scriptural perspective. Derived from the Latin "integer," it implies a wholeness or completeness that is fundamentally connected to the character of God. It is this character that is often described in the Old Testament with terms like "righteousness," "justice," and "faithfulness." The Bible abounds with exhortations for believers to walk in integrity (Proverbs 10:9, 11:3). But what does it really mean to follow the pathway of integrity in the context of biblical Christianity?

The Theological Underpinnings of Integrity

Understanding integrity from a Scriptural viewpoint first necessitates an understanding of God's character. God is described as being righteous (Deuteronomy 32:4) and faithful (Isaiah 25:1). If the believer is called to be "holy as God is holy" (1 Peter 1:15-16), then an innate part of this call is to cultivate a life of integrity. It is not merely a moral or ethical construct but is intrinsically tied to the very nature of God.

Integrity as Exemplified in Biblical Narratives

Key biblical figures offer us valuable insights into the practicalities of living a life of integrity. Take, for example, Joseph in Genesis 39. When faced with the temptation to commit adultery with Potiphar's wife, he didn't merely decline but fled from the situation. His integrity was born from his awareness of God's presence: "How can I do this great wickedness and sin against God?" (Genesis 39:9, ESV). Joseph's integrity wasn't merely personal virtue but a virtue cultivated in the soil of reverence for God.

Integrity in the Wisdom Literature

The book of Proverbs, particularly, underscores the value of integrity. Proverbs 10:9 states, "Whoever walks in integrity walks securely, but he who makes his ways crooked will be found out" (ESV). The verse beautifully contrasts integrity with deceit, showing that integrity results in a secure, straightforward life, devoid of the constant fear of exposure that accompanies deceitfulness.

The Epistles and Integrity

Apostle Paul's letters provide a New Testament framework for understanding integrity. In 2 Corinthians 1:12, Paul notes, "For our boast is this, the testimony of our conscience, that we behaved in the world with simplicity and godly sincerity, not by earthly wisdom but by the grace of God, and supremely so toward you" (ESV). This verse highlights how integrity is connected to a clear conscience and godly sincerity, attributes that believers are exhorted to emulate.

Practical Applications for Daily Living

1. **Biblical Study**: Diligent study of the Scriptures using a historical-grammatical method allows us to understand the original intent of the text, thus facilitating a clearer understanding of the moral and ethical guidelines set forth.
2. **Prayer**: Prayerful communication with God for wisdom and guidance can help in making decisions that align with a life of integrity.
3. **Ethical Choices**: The mundane choices we make in our everyday life—whether in business, relationships, or personal behavior—should reflect integrity. For instance, honesty in financial matters is a direct reflection of one's commitment to godly integrity (Luke 16:10-11).
4. **Accountability**: Having an accountability partner or being part of a Bible-based community can serve as safeguards on the pathway of integrity (James 5:16).
5. **Moral Vigilance**: Integrity requires constant vigilance against compromise. A regular examination of one's life in the light of Scripture can aid in this (2 Corinthians 13:5).

The pathway of integrity is not an easy one, but it is deeply rooted in the very character of God. It transcends ethical moralism and taps into the abundant life that Jesus promised to those who follow Him (John 10:10). For the believer, integrity is not merely an external attribute but a manifestation of inner spiritual health. It provides a stable, secure pathway in a world that often celebrates duplicity and compromise. Hence, the pursuit of integrity is not optional but foundational for anyone desiring to live a life that glorifies God.

By faithfully adhering to God's teachings and continuously seeking His guidance, believers can tread the pathway of integrity. In doing so, they do not merely live virtuous lives but reflect the very nature of God to a world that desperately needs to see authentic Christianity in action.

God's Truth as Moral Compass

In a postmodern society that increasingly relativizes truth and morality, the believer is often left bewildered, caught between cultural norms and Scriptural mandates. The necessity of having an unchanging standard of truth as a moral compass has never been more imperative. This essay aims to elucidate how God's truth serves as the ultimate moral compass for believers, providing a secure framework for ethical decisions and spiritual growth.

The Foundation of Moral Compass: God Himself

Before discussing God's truth, it is crucial to understand that truth emanates from God's own character. Jehovah is described as the "God of truth" (Psalm 31:5, ESV), indicating that truth is not a concept God ascribes to but an attribute He embodies. Therefore, when we talk about God's truth, we are delving into His character, which is eternally unchanging (Malachi 3:6).

The Source of God's Truth: Scripture

For the believer, the Bible is the primary source where God's truth is revealed. All Scripture is "breathed out by God and profitable for teaching, for reproof, for correction, and for training in righteousness" (2 Timothy 3:16, ESV). The written Word of God stands as the unchanging truth that navigates us through the complexities of life. Being based on the objective historical-grammatical method of interpretation, we understand that Scripture's role as a moral compass is not a cultural or epochal construct but an eternal standard.

The Pervasiveness of Relative Morality and the Need for an Absolute Standard

The modern era's intellectual climate often leans toward moral relativism, where truth is subjective and varies from person to person. However, the inherent problem with this approach is its inability to provide a stable foundation for morality. If all truth is relative, then the notions of justice, goodness, and righteousness lose their meaning. That's where the importance of an unchanging, absolute standard comes into play. God's truth offers an anchor in a sea of moral ambiguity.

Case Studies: Moral Dilemmas and God's Truth

Let's consider a few practical scenarios where the believer could utilize God's truth as a moral compass:

1. **Business Ethics**: In a setting where dishonesty could lead to personal gain, Scriptures like Proverbs 11:1 ("A false balance is an abomination to the Lord, but a just weight is his delight," ESV) provide a clear moral directive.

2. **Relationships**: In personal relationships, the teachings of Jesus on love, forgiveness, and reconciliation (Matthew 5:43-48; 18:21-22) offer a blueprint for navigating complex relational dynamics.

3. **Social Justice**: The biblical mandate for justice (Micah 6:8) and care for the marginalized (James 1:27) offers believers guidance on social issues that are often politically charged and complex.

Practical Steps for Utilizing God's Truth as a Moral Compass

1. **Immerse in the Word**: A routine study of God's Word, understood literally and within its historical and grammatical context, is foundational.

2. **Prayerful Guidance**: Constant prayer for wisdom and understanding can illuminate the Scriptures and help in applying them to real-life scenarios (James 1:5).

3. **Community Support**: Being part of a like-minded Christian community can serve as an additional layer of guidance and accountability (Hebrews 10:24-25).

4. **Holistic Application**: God's truth should be applied not just in "spiritual" matters but in every aspect of life, be it career, education, or politics (Colossians 3:17).

The notion that God's truth serves as a moral compass is deeply rooted in the inherent character of God and is articulated through His revealed Word. It offers an unwavering standard in a world that increasingly shuns moral absolutes. By aligning ourselves with God's truth, we not only navigate the complexities of life but also mirror God's character, glorifying Him in the process.

Through a diligent study of Scripture, prayer, and community support, a believer can robustly employ God's truth as a moral compass. This does not merely offer an ethical framework but serves to fulfill the ultimate goal of the Christian life—conformity to the image of Christ (Romans 8:29), the embodiment of truth Himself (John 14:6). Therefore, the pursuit of truth is not just an intellectual endeavor but a spiritual quest that impacts every facet of the believer's life, offering guidance, stability, and a means to glorify God in a fallen world.

The Link Between Truth and Obedience

Truth and obedience are inextricably connected in the Christian life. Often, we compartmentalize these virtues, treating them as separate entities. Yet, Scripture abundantly reveals that understanding God's truth should lead us to obedience, and through obedience, we gain a fuller understanding of God's truth. This essay aims to elucidate the relationship between these two crucial aspects of Christian spirituality.

The Inherent Nature of God's Truth

The foundation of any discussion on truth must begin with God. Jehovah is described as the God of truth (Psalm 31:5), and His Word is truth (John 17:17). The understanding of truth within a biblical framework is never separated from the character of God. It is not a neutral or abstract concept but is rooted in who God is and what He has revealed.

The Mandate for Obedience

The mandate for obedience is equally rooted in God's character. The Old Testament is replete with calls to obey Jehovah, keeping His statutes and commands (Deuteronomy 11:26-28). In the New Testament, Jesus Himself says, "If you love me, you will keep my commandments" (John 14:15, ESV). Clearly, obedience is not a legalistic demand but a relational expectation rooted in love and reverence for God.

The Scriptural Nexus Between Truth and Obedience

The Bible does not treat truth and obedience as isolated virtues but links them in several significant ways.

1. **Wisdom and Understanding**: Proverbs 2:6 notes that the Lord gives wisdom, and from His mouth come knowledge and understanding. Obedience to God's laws is described as wisdom and understanding (Deuteronomy 4:6). Hence, understanding God's truth through Scripture grants us the wisdom required for obedience.

2. **Freedom Through Truth**: Jesus taught that knowing the truth would set us free (John 8:32). This freedom is not merely intellectual or emotional but manifests as freedom from sin, leading us to a life of obedience (Romans 6:17-18).

3. **Evidence of Love**: Jesus links love for Him with keeping His commandments (John 14:15). The apostle John echoes this in 1 John 5:3: "For this is the love of God, that we keep his commandments." Truth informs our understanding of who God is, which in turn shapes our love for Him and manifests as obedience.

4. **Fruitfulness**: In John 15:1-11, Jesus describes Himself as the vine and believers as the branches. Abiding in Him, which implies knowing His truth, leads to fruitfulness, an expression of obedience.

Obedience as an Avenue to Understanding Truth

Not only does understanding truth lead to obedience, but the pathway is also reciprocal. Obedience fosters a greater understanding of God's truth. Jesus promises in John 7:17 that anyone who chooses to do God's will understand whether His teaching comes from God. Through the act of obeying God's Word, believers find themselves drawn into a deeper understanding of divine truths.

Implications for Christian Living

1. **Scriptural Study**: Understanding the link between truth and obedience reinforces the importance of studying the Scriptures, which are the source of divine truth.

2. **Prayerful Obedience**: We need the wisdom to apply God's truth in our daily lives. Prayer becomes a critical factor, as James 1:5 tells us that God will generously give wisdom to those who ask.

3. **Reflective Evaluation**: Continual examination of our lives to see if our actions align with biblical truth is vital. This requires a commitment to ongoing repentance and growth in obedience.

4. **Community Accountability**: As members of the body of Christ, we should exhort and encourage one another in the truth (Hebrews 10:24-25). Community becomes a forum for both learning truth and practicing obedience.

The relationship between truth and obedience is cyclical rather than linear. Understanding truth motivates obedience, and practicing obedience engenders a deeper understanding of truth. Both emanate from God's character and are revealed in His Word. Moreover, they intersect in the person of Jesus Christ, who is the way, the truth, and the life (John 14:6). His life exemplifies perfect obedience to God's will and serves as our model (Hebrews 5:8-9).

Therefore, separating truth from obedience or vice versa results in a fragmented understanding of Christian discipleship. The pursuit of God's truth is not merely an intellectual endeavor, but it calls for a transformational obedience that impacts every facet of our lives. In a world often marred by deception and disobedience, understanding and applying the link between truth and obedience is not only essential for personal spiritual growth but is also critical for the collective witness of the Church.

In the quest for spiritual growth and a deeper relationship with God, the link between truth and obedience emerges as a foundational and transformative concept. This connection is not only profound but also practical, offering believers a clear path to living out their faith in an authentic and meaningful way. Throughout the pages of Scripture, from the Old Testament to the New, the importance of aligning one's life with divine truth is a recurring theme. In this exploration, we will delve into this crucial link between truth and obedience, drawing insights from both the Old and New Testaments.

The Foundation in Old Testament Wisdom

To grasp the significance of the link between truth and obedience, we must first turn our attention to the wisdom literature of the Old Testament, particularly the book of Proverbs. Proverbs 23:23 succinctly encapsulates the essence of this connection: "Buy truth, and do not sell it; buy wisdom, instruction, and understanding." Here, truth is portrayed as a valuable commodity, something worth acquiring and holding onto at all costs.

In the context of Proverbs, truth encompasses not only factual accuracy but also moral integrity and divine wisdom. To "buy truth" implies a deliberate and intentional pursuit of God's wisdom and moral guidance. This pursuit is not passive but requires an active engagement with God's Word and a willingness to align one's life with His truth.

The link between truth and obedience in Proverbs becomes even more explicit when we consider the broader themes of wisdom and righteousness. The entire book is a guide to wise and righteous living, and wisdom is intricately connected to the fear of the Lord (Proverbs 1:7). The fear of the Lord is, in essence, an acknowledgment of His authority and a recognition of His truth as the ultimate standard.

In Proverbs 3:5-6, we read, "Trust in Jehovah with all your heart, and do not lean on your own understanding. In all your ways acknowledge him, and he will make straight your paths." This verse underscores the importance of trust and obedience to God's guidance. Acknowledging God in all our ways is an act of aligning ourselves with His truth, allowing His wisdom to direct our paths.

The Teachings of Jesus

The link between truth and obedience finds its most profound expression in the teachings of Jesus. In John 14:6, Jesus declares, "I am the way, and the truth, and the life. No one comes to the Father except through me." Here, Jesus identifies Himself as the embodiment of truth. He is not merely a teacher of truth but Truth personified.

To follow Jesus is to walk in truth, and this walk necessitates obedience to His teachings. In John 14:15, Jesus says, "If you love me, you will keep my commandments." Love for Jesus is intimately connected to obedience to His commands. It is through obedience that we demonstrate our love for Him and align ourselves with the truth He embodies.

The parable of the wise and foolish builders in Matthew 7:24-27 further illustrates the link between truth and obedience. Jesus tells of two builders—one who hears His words and acts on them (obedience) and another who hears but does not obey. The wise builder's house stands firm in the face of storms, symbolizing a life anchored in truth and obedience, while the foolish builder's house crumbles, representing a life built on disobedience.

The Apostle John's Emphasis on Truth and Obedience

The apostle John, in his writings, places a strong emphasis on the connection between truth and obedience. In 1 John 2:3-6, he states:

"And by this, we know that we have come to know him if we keep his commandments. Whoever says 'I know him' but does not keep his commandments is a liar, and the truth is not in him, but whoever keeps his word, in him truly the love of God is perfected. By this, we may know that we are in him: whoever says he abides in him ought to walk in the same way in which he walked."

John's words are clear and uncompromising: knowing God is inseparable from obeying His commandments. The link between truth and obedience is evident in the assertion that love for God is perfected through obedience to His Word. Obedience, then, becomes a tangible expression of our relationship with God and our alignment with His truth.

John's writings also emphasize the transformative power of truth and obedience. In 1 John 3:2-3, he says, "Beloved, we are God's children now, and what we will be has not yet appeared; but we know that when he appears we shall be like him because we shall see him as he is. And everyone who thus hopes in him purifies himself as he is pure." Here, the link between seeing God as He is (truth) and purifying oneself (obedience) is evident. The pursuit of holiness and purity is a direct result of aligning one's life with the truth of God's character.

The Call to Discipleship

Understanding the link between truth and obedience is not merely an intellectual exercise but a call to discipleship. In Matthew 28:18-20, known as the Great Commission, Jesus instructs His disciples to make more disciples of all nations, baptizing them in the name of the Father, Son, and Holy Spirit, and teaching them to obey everything He commanded. The heart of discipleship is obedience to the teachings of Jesus.

The apostle Paul echoes this sentiment in Romans 1:5, where he speaks of "the obedience of faith among all the Gentiles for his name's sake." Faith is not divorced from obedience but inherently linked to it. True faith in Christ manifests itself through obedience to His lordship.

The Fruit of Truthful Obedience

As we explore the link between truth and obedience, we discover that it bears abundant fruit in the life of a believer. Obedience to God's truth leads to a transformed character marked by righteousness, love, and holiness. It fosters a deep intimacy with God as we align our will with His. Obedience also results in a life of purpose and fulfillment, as we live out the divine calling and mission He has placed on our lives.

Moreover, obedience to truth strengthens our witness to the world. When the world sees the transformative power of God's truth in our lives, it becomes a compelling testimony to the reality of Christ. Our obedience becomes a shining light in a world often shrouded in darkness.

In conclusion, the link between truth and obedience is a central theme in Scripture and an essential aspect of the Christian faith. It is a call to align our lives with the unchanging truth of God's Word and to walk in obedience to His commands. This link is not a burden but a source of abundant life, transforming us into the image of Christ and empowering us to fulfill our divine calling as disciples of the Truth Himself.

PROVERBS 23:23 Buy Truth—Do Not Sell It

The Intrinsic Value of Truth

The aphorism "Buy truth—do not sell it" found in Proverbs 23:23 is a profound declaration of the intrinsic value of truth in the life of a believer. This wisdom text does not intend for us to understand "buying" and "selling" in a commercial sense, but rather metaphorically, signifying the extent of commitment required in pursuing truth. The directive underscores the immeasurable worth of truth and places it in stark contrast with anything transient or deceptive. This essay seeks to explore the multi-faceted dimensions of the intrinsic value of truth, as revealed in Scripture, and its implications for Christian living.

The Truth of God's Word

The Bible itself is the ultimate source of truth. The Psalmist exclaims, "The sum of your word is truth" (Psalm 119:160, ESV). This truth is not a philosophical concept but is embodied in the nature and character of God. Jehovah is described as a God "who cannot lie" (Titus 1:2). Thus, when we speak of buying truth, the first purchase, metaphorically speaking, is a commitment to the divine revelation found in the Scriptures.

The Incorruptible Nature of Truth

Truth stands in opposition to falsehood, deception, and all forms of moral and intellectual corruption. Its intrinsic value lies in its incorruptible nature. Unlike material possessions that can decay or be stolen, truth endures. Jesus Christ emphasized this when He declared, "Heaven and earth will pass away, but my words will not pass away" (Matthew 24:35, ESV).

The Cost of Acquiring Truth

To "buy truth" implies a cost, a sacrificial dimension. Jesus spoke of the kingdom of heaven as a treasure hidden in a field, for which a man sold all he had to buy that field (Matthew 13:44). This parable illustrates the worth of divine truth and the cost one should be willing to pay to acquire it. This could mean rejecting societal norms, cutting off relationships, or foregoing personal gains that stand in opposition to God's truth.

Why Not Sell It?

The text also includes a firm directive: "do not sell it." The truth is not to be compromised or given away for momentary advantages. Its intrinsic value makes it non-negotiable. The early church provides numerous examples of saints who did not "sell" the truth even when faced with persecution and death (Acts 4:19-20; Revelation 2:10).

The Value of Associated Virtues

The verse doesn't stop at buying truth but extends to wisdom, instruction, and understanding. These are not separate entities but closely related facets of a life lived in alignment with God's will. They are, in essence, the operationalization of truth in different dimensions of human experience.

Implications for Christian Living

1. **Unwavering Commitment**: The unwavering commitment to truth must manifest in our beliefs and practices. It should affect our choices, influence our morality, and guide our interactions with others.

2. **Discernment**: In an age teeming with information, not all that is presented as truth genuinely is. A strong commitment to biblical truth equips us with the discernment needed to navigate these complexities (Hebrews 4:12).

3. **Witnessing and Testimony**: The commitment to never "sell" truth has implications for evangelism. The Gospel message must be proclaimed in its fullness, without dilution or compromise.

4. **Personal Transformation**: The pursuit and application of truth are transformative. As Paul notes, we are to be "transformed by the renewal of [our] mind" (Romans 12:2), a process facilitated through engaging deeply with divine truth.

5. **Community Building**: A collective commitment to truth within the body of Christ serves to build a community founded on trust, integrity, and love (Ephesians 4:15-16).

The intrinsic value of truth as depicted in Proverbs 23:23 is immeasurable. It is a treasure that requires an intentional and often sacrificial commitment to acquire and maintain. The virtues associated with it—wisdom, instruction, understanding—are complementary assets that enrich our spiritual journey. Selling or compromising this truth is not an option for the believer; its value far outweighs any temporary gains or conveniences.

The call to "buy truth and do not sell it" is not just ancient wisdom but a timely mandate for contemporary Christians. In an era marked by relativism, compromise, and superficiality, the profound value of truth beckons us to a higher standard. Adhering to this standard is not merely a personal preference but an imperative rooted in the character of God and His revelation to humanity. In recognizing the inestimable value of truth, we find ourselves aligned with the very heart of God, positioned for spiritual growth and effective service in His kingdom.

The Cost of Acquiring Wisdom

Wisdom is a prized possession in the Christian life, one that Scripture exhorts us to pursue vigorously. It transcends knowledge and understanding, guiding us not merely in what we know but in how we apply that knowledge in real-life situations. Proverbs 4:7 asserts, "The beginning of wisdom is this: Get wisdom, and whatever you get, get insight" (ESV). The urgency of this verse signifies that wisdom is not an optional or peripheral pursuit but a critical necessity for living a godly life. However, acquiring wisdom is not without its costs. This essay aims to explore the multifaceted costs of gaining wisdom and why those costs are justified.

The Intrinsic Value of Wisdom

To fully grasp the cost, we must first understand the value of the product. Wisdom is so esteemed in Scripture that it is likened to precious metals and gemstones. Proverbs 3:14-15 says, "for the gain from [wisdom] is better than gain from silver and her profit better than gold. She is more precious than jewels, and nothing you desire can compare with her" (ESV). The essence of wisdom carries eternal implications; it's not just about worldly success but about pleasing God and living in harmony with His statutes.

Costs of Acquiring Wisdom

Time and Dedication

Wisdom doesn't come instantly; it requires an investment of time and sincere dedication. Time spent studying Scripture, praying for wisdom (James 1:5), and seeking godly counsel are integral components of this investment.

Sacrifice

There is a sacrificial element in the pursuit of wisdom. You may have to forsake worldly pleasures, ideologies, or relationships that do not align with godly wisdom. Just as one would sell everything to buy a field containing a treasure (Matthew 13:44), so must one be willing to sacrifice for wisdom.

Humility

True wisdom entails acknowledging one's limitations and weaknesses. This is a form of cost, as human pride often hinders the path to wisdom. Proverbs 11:2 states, "When pride comes, then comes disgrace, but with the humble is wisdom" (ESV).

Trials and Suffering

Wisdom is often acquired through the furnace of affliction. While God didn't design suffering to foster growth, He allows it to teach humanity an object lesson about the importance of His sovereignty. These experiences, while not pleasant, contribute to a well-rounded wisdom that theoretical knowledge alone cannot provide.

Obedience

Obedience to God's commands is another cost of gaining wisdom. It might be difficult and countercultural, but obedience in the form of ethical living, maintaining purity, and exercising integrity are prerequisites for gaining wisdom. The Scriptures confirm that the "fear of Jehovah is the beginning of wisdom" (Proverbs 9:10, ESV).

The Unquantifiable Returns

The rewards of acquiring wisdom far outweigh its costs. Wisdom offers a life led in alignment with God's will, promises peace, and provides the ability to make decisions that result in blessings rather than calamity. As Proverbs 3:17 reveals, "Her ways are ways of pleasantness, and all her paths are peace" (ESV). These benefits are not just for the here and now; they have eternal significance, leading us toward a life that honors God and prepares us for eternity.

Wisdom and the Community

Wisdom isn't solely for individual betterment; its ripple effects benefit families, churches, and communities. A wise person is better equipped to counsel others, lead effectively, and foster an atmosphere of harmony. Wisdom cultivates a spirit of unity and collective growth, serving as a cornerstone for building strong communities of faith.

Modern-Day Implications

The pursuit of wisdom is especially crucial in an age characterized by moral relativism, a plethora of conflicting ideologies, and widespread deception. The cost of acquiring wisdom may seem daunting in such a cultural climate, but its necessity cannot be overstated. In a world quick to offer "quick fixes" and easy answers, the laborious path to wisdom may seem archaic, yet it remains the only sure way to a fulfilling and God-honoring life.

The path to acquiring wisdom is not without its challenges and costs. It requires an investment of time, the humility to admit our limitations, the courage to sacrifice worldly comforts, and a steadfast commitment to obedience. Yet, the costs are not burdensome when compared to the immense and eternal value that wisdom offers. The wisdom that comes from God, who is its ultimate source, enables us to navigate the complexities of life in a manner that brings glory to Him while providing us with a sense of peace, purpose, and eternal perspective.

In recognizing the value of wisdom and committing ourselves to bear the cost of acquiring it, we not only enrich our lives but also contribute to the larger purpose of God's plan for humanity. Our pursuit of wisdom, while costly, is an investment with eternal dividends, aligning us more closely with God's character and preparing us for effective service in His kingdom.

The Dangers of Trading Truth

The Bible unequivocally places a high premium on truth. Jesus Himself proclaimed, "I am the way, and the truth, and the life" (John 14:6, ESV). Truth is not just a concept or an abstract principle; it's a person—Jesus Christ. Nevertheless, we find that truth is frequently bartered, diluted, or outright rejected in society and, sadly, even within Christian communities. The danger of trading truth for falsehood is immense, affecting not just our temporal existence but our eternal destiny. This essay will explore the dangers inherent in trading truth for lies, half-truths, or convenient narratives.

Biblical Perspective on Truth

Before delving into the dangers, it's crucial to establish the Biblical stance on truth. The Scriptures portray truth as absolute, unchanging, and divinely originated. The Psalmist declares, "The sum of your word is truth, and every one of your righteous rules endures forever" (Psalm 119:160, ESV). Jehovah, the God of the Bible, is a God of truth, devoid of iniquity (Deuteronomy 32:4). Hence, any departure from truth is a departure from God Himself.

Dangers of Trading Truth

Eroding Moral Foundation

When truth is compromised, the moral foundation upon which individuals and societies are built begins to erode. Proverbs 14:34 observes, "Righteousness exalts a nation, but sin is a reproach to any people" (ESV). The rejection of truth leads to moral relativism, where ethics become fluid and subjective, resulting in societal decay.

Impaired Spiritual Discernment

Compromising on truth dulls spiritual discernment. The Scriptures assert that the word of God is sharper than a two-edged sword, discerning thoughts and intentions of the heart (Hebrews 4:12). When truth is traded for lies, individuals lose their ability to discern between right and wrong, good and evil, thereby making them susceptible to deceptive doctrines.

Risk of False Teachings

The Apostle Paul warned Timothy that a time would come when people would not endure sound teaching but would accumulate teachers to suit their own passions (2 Timothy 4:3). When truth is devalued, falsehood gains currency, giving rise to heresies and false teachings that lead people astray.

Loss of Witness

The credibility of the Christian community is at stake when truth is compromised. Jesus prayed for His followers, "Sanctify them in the truth; your word is truth" (John 17:17, ESV). A community that trades truth loses its sanctifying influence in the world, thus weakening its witness.

Eternal Ramifications

The gravest danger in trading truth is the risk of eternal separation from God. Jesus said, "And you will know the truth, and the truth will set you free" (John 8:32, ESV). Conversely, living in falsehood enslaves and leads to eternal damnation. The Apostle Paul warned about those who "exchanged the truth about God for a lie" (Romans 1:25, ESV), illustrating the eternal consequences of rejecting truth.

The Allure of Falsehood

Given these dangers, why is there an inclination to trade truth? The reasons are manifold: societal pressure, personal convenience, avoidance of conflict, or even ignorance. However, the underlying issue is often a rebellious heart that seeks autonomy from God's sovereignty. This yearning for independence results in the willingness to compromise or reject truth, even at a high cost.

The Unyielding Stance on Truth

The Scriptures do not grant us the luxury of selective adherence to truth. The Apostle John exhorts us to "walk in the truth" (3 John 1:4, ESV), and the Psalmist resolves to "speak the truth in [his] heart" (Psalm 15:2, ESV). The objective Historical-Grammatical method of interpretation, which emphasizes the literal understanding of Scripture, also underscores the necessity of holding to the truth in its unadulterated form.

Trading truth comes with a heavy price tag, including the erosion of moral foundations, the corruption of spiritual discernment, the risk of false teachings, a weakened witness, and, most severely, eternal ramifications. The sobering reality is that when we compromise on truth, we are, in essence, distancing ourselves from God, who is the very embodiment of truth.

We are living through an object lesson that shows us the importance of adhering to the sovereignty of God and not relying on human wisdom. In a world fraught with confusion, misinformation, and deception, our commitment to truth must be unwavering. Our stand on truth should not be determined by its popularity or its ease but by its divine origin and eternal significance.

The dangers of trading truth should propel us into diligent study, fervent prayer, and vigilant watchfulness. In a world where truth is increasingly sidelined or redefined, we must uphold it, defend it, and live it out, regardless of the cost. Only then can we hope to navigate the complexities of life with integrity, contribute positively to the Christian community, and fulfill our ultimate purpose of glorifying God.

The Lasting Investment in Integrity

Integrity is one of the most invaluable assets a Christian can possess. It's not just a character trait; it's a lifestyle—a conscious commitment to align one's thoughts, words, and actions with God's revealed truth in Scripture. The Psalmist, King David, displayed a profound understanding of integrity when he resolved: "I will ponder the way that is blameless. Oh when will you come to me? I will walk with integrity of heart within my house" (Psalm 101:2, ESV). The concept of integrity is not only deeply rooted in the Bible, but it also offers lasting benefits, both temporal and eternal. This essay aims to delineate the importance of investing in a life of integrity, drawing from a literal interpretation of Scripture.

Biblical Foundation of Integrity

Integrity comes from a Hebrew term, 'tamim,' which means "complete" or "whole." Jehovah, the God of the Bible, requires His followers to be complete or whole in their devotion to Him. The Book of Proverbs asserts, "The integrity of the upright guides them, but the crookedness of the treacherous destroys them" (Proverbs 11:3, ESV). Integrity, therefore, serves as a moral compass, aligning us with the will of God.

The Temporal Rewards of Integrity

Favor and Honor

Proverbs 3:3-4 exclaims, "Let not steadfast love and faithfulness forsake you; bind them around your neck; write them on the tablet of your heart. So you will find favor and good success in the sight of God and man" (ESV). One of the immediate, temporal rewards of integrity is favor from both God and men. This favor can manifest in various aspects of life such as relationships, business, and ministry.

Stability in Times of Trial

In a world where circumstances can change in an instant, integrity provides a stable foundation. The Psalmist proclaims, "He will not be afraid of bad news; his heart is firm, trusting in Jehovah. His heart is steady; he will not be afraid" (Psalm 112:7-8, ESV). The person of integrity trusts in God's promises, resulting in a steadfast spirit that is not easily moved by external situations.

Fulfilling Relationships

Integrity begets trust, and trust is fundamental to any relationship. Whether in marriage, friendship, or community, a person known for integrity will foster deeper, more meaningful connections.

The Eternal Rewards of Integrity

Divine Recognition

The ultimate reward for integrity is not in this life but in the eternal presence of God. Jesus declared, "Well done, good and faithful servant. You have been faithful over a little; I will set you over much. Enter into the joy of your master" (Matthew 25:21, ESV). Integrity on earth equates to eternal commendation from the Lord.

Eternal Inheritance

The Scriptures talk about an inheritance that is "imperishable, undefiled, and unfading, kept in heaven for you" (1 Peter 1:4, ESV). This inheritance is promised to those who, among other virtues, maintain their integrity in their walk with God.

The Cost of Integrity

While the rewards are immense, the path to integrity is not without cost. Often, it requires standing against societal norms, confronting sin, and sacrificing immediate gratification for eternal gain. Integrity may cost you friendships, job opportunities, and social standing. But, as the Apostle Paul emphasizes, "I consider that the sufferings of this present time are not worth comparing with the glory that is to be revealed to us" (Romans 8:18, ESV).

The Irreplaceability of Integrity

In a world filled with temporary and perishable goods, integrity is one asset that neither moth nor rust can destroy (Matthew 6:19-20). You may lose wealth, health, or relationships, but integrity—once firmly established—is eternal. It's an investment that continues to yield dividends in this life and in the life to come.

In the final analysis, investing in integrity is a commitment to align one's life entirely with the truth of God as revealed in Scripture. It is a choice to live a life that is pleasing to God, whether or not it's convenient or popular. It's the practice of making decisions not based on their immediate pay-off but on their alignment with eternal principles.

We are learning an object lesson that living apart from the sovereignty of God and the truth of His Word is detrimental. And conversely, aligning ourselves with His truth and walking in integrity has far-reaching implications, extending from our personal well-being to the health of our communities, and ultimately, to our eternal destiny.

As we navigate the intricacies of life, may our investment in integrity serve as a lasting testament to our devotion to Jehovah. We must remember that our stand on integrity should not be determined by its popularity or its ease but by its divine origin and eternal significance. This commitment to integrity not only enriches our earthly journey but assures our eternal placement in the presence of our Heavenly Father.

JOHN 4:23 Worship the Father in Spirit and Truth

Defining Authentic Worship

In John 4:23, Jesus tells the Samaritan woman, "But the hour is coming, and is now here, when the true worshipers will worship the Father in spirit and truth, for the Father is seeking such people to worship him" (ESV). This statement is profound, especially coming from Jesus Christ, who not only perfectly modeled authentic worship but also outlined the essential elements required for it—worship in "spirit and truth." What does it mean to worship Jehovah in spirit and truth? This essay aims to explore the biblical doctrine of authentic worship based on a literal interpretation of Scripture, focusing on John 4:23.

Contextual Overview

To grasp the depth of this statement, we must first understand the context in which Jesus spoke these words. He was addressing a Samaritan woman, a representative of a group who were considered heretics by the Jews. They had a flawed concept of worship, both in location (Mount Gerizim versus Jerusalem) and form. Jesus' statement was revolutionary; it redefined worship from being merely ritualistic or locational to something deeper, transcendent, and universal.

Worship in Spirit

The Meaning of "Spirit"

The term "spirit" refers to the innermost part of man, the seat of emotions and will. It is the very core of a person's being. Worshiping "in spirit" means engaging in worship with one's whole heart, sincerely and genuinely.

Emotional Engagement

Worshiping in spirit isn't a call for emotionalism but for emotional engagement. The Psalms are replete with a range of emotions expressed toward God, from joy to sorrow, from awe to love. Emotions, while not the root of worship, are an integral part of the worship experience.

Intentionality and Focus

Worshiping in spirit also implies intentionality and focus. Our spirit should be engaged in the act of worship. This means worship isn't accidental or superficial but a conscious, deliberate act.

Worship in Truth

The Meaning of "Truth"

Worshiping in "truth" means aligning our worship with the revealed Word of God in the Scriptures. Truth here is not merely a philosophical concept; it's the concrete, objective truth revealed in the Bible.

Conformance to Doctrine

Our worship must be grounded in correct biblical doctrine. There is no room for subjective or relativistic interpretations of what worship should be. This eliminates practices and beliefs not aligned with Scripture.

Authenticity

Worshiping in truth also requires that we be genuine. Jesus rebuked the Pharisees for their hypocritical worship: "This people honors me with their lips, but their heart is far from me; in vain do they worship me, teaching as doctrines the commandments of men" (Matthew 15:8-9, ESV).

The Confluence of Spirit and Truth

Worship is complete only when spirit and truth intersect. One without the other is inadequate. Worshiping in spirit alone can lead to emotionalism devoid of substance, while worshiping in truth alone can result in a dry, intellectual exercise.

The Objective of Worship

The ultimate goal of worship is not self-satisfaction or emotional experience. Rather, it is the exaltation of God. As the Apostle Paul writes, "So, whether you eat or drink, or whatever you do, do all to the glory of God" (1 Corinthians 10:31, ESV).

The Corporate Aspect

While personal worship is crucial, the New Testament emphasizes the importance of corporate worship—believers coming together to exalt God as a community. The early church "devoted themselves to the apostles' teaching and the fellowship, to the breaking of bread and the prayers" (Acts 2:42, ESV).

Implications for Today

Our object lesson—living independently of God—shows us the dire consequences of deviating from the divine pattern set by Scripture, including in worship. It reaffirms the need for spirit and truth in our approach to worshiping Jehovah. As our culture leans more into subjectivism and emotionalism, grounding our worship in both spirit and truth is more crucial than ever.

Worshiping Jehovah in spirit and truth is not an optional preference but a divine requirement. This worship involves an emotional engagement that is grounded in theological accuracy, centered on God, and executed both individually and corporately. Only then do we meet the criteria Jesus set for true worshipers, aligning ourselves with the Father's desire for such worship and, thereby, fulfilling our very purpose for existence—to glorify God.

Authentic worship is an investment in our spiritual health and eternal future. It draws us closer to Jehovah, nourishes our soul, and equips us for godly living. It's a commitment to the most profound relationship we can ever have—that with our Creator. May our lives be a continuous offering of worship in spirit and truth, fulfilling our divine calling and anticipating our eternal fellowship with God.

The Role of Spirit in Worship

The subject of worship is critical in the life of a Christian, and the Bible provides us with an array of teachings on how worship should be conducted. While Jesus outlines the blueprint for worshiping "in spirit and truth" in John 4:23, understanding the role of the 'spirit' in worship can sometimes be an area where many have differing opinions. What does it mean to worship God "in spirit?" This paper aims to expound on the role of the spirit in worship based on a literal interpretation of Scripture.

The Meaning of 'Spirit' in Worship

When Jesus speaks of worshiping "in spirit," the term "spirit" represents the core, the essence of our inner being. It refers to the seat of our emotions, intellect, and will—the true 'us' behind the physical shell. Worshiping "in spirit" entails engaging in worship at the most fundamental level of who we are. It means worshiping genuinely, from the heart.

Emotional Engagement vs Emotionalism

Worshiping in spirit involves emotional engagement, but it should not be confused with emotionalism. Emotional engagement signifies an authentic relationship with Jehovah, where one's feelings—be they awe, joy, or gratitude—are a natural by-product of understanding God's character and works. On the other hand, emotionalism is the manipulation or orchestration of emotions for the sake of the emotional experience itself. This doesn't honor God and often misleads people into thinking that emotional highs are equivalent to spiritual maturity.

The Element of Sincerity

Sincerity is at the core of worshiping in spirit. God does not look at the outward appearance but at the heart (1 Samuel 16:7). When the Israelites were rebuked by Jehovah through the prophets, one of the core issues was their lack of sincerity in worship. They followed rituals but lacked a genuine relationship with God, making their worship unacceptable (Isaiah 1:11-17).

Intentionality and Focus

Worshiping in spirit is not something that happens accidentally. It requires intentional focus and purpose. When Peter wrote, "Prepare your minds for action" (1 Peter 1:13, ESV), he was emphasizing the need for Christians to be alert and focused in their spiritual duties, including worship. Worshiping in spirit means to consciously direct our innermost being towards adoration, praise, and submission to God.

The Importance of Humility

Another vital aspect of worshiping in spirit is the element of humility. Worship is an act of submission to Jehovah, acknowledging His sovereignty and our dependence on Him. The Pharisee in Luke 18:9-14 stands as an example of how not to approach God; his prayer was more an exaltation of himself rather than a humble approach to Jehovah.

Worship as a Lifestyle

Paul encourages believers to "present your bodies as a living sacrifice, holy and acceptable to God, which is your spiritual worship" (Romans 12:1, ESV). Worshiping in spirit is not confined to a Sunday service or a specific religious event; it is a lifestyle. It encompasses our attitudes, actions, and daily living. Worship becomes a continuous act when our spirit is consistently attuned to God.

The Role of the Holy Spirit

It's essential to clarify that the term "spirit" in John 4:23 is about our human spirit, not the Holy Spirit. While we are not indwelt by the Holy Spirit, Scripture teaches that we are guided by the Spirit-inspired Word of God. Our worship is informed and directed by the teachings of Scripture, making it an act that glorifies God.

Personal and Corporate Worship

Worshiping in spirit is not limited to personal worship; it extends to corporate worship. When the church gathers, collective worship should also be in spirit. Each member contributes to the atmosphere of worship, and when each person is worshiping in spirit, it creates a setting where God is genuinely glorified.

Worshiping "in spirit" is an imperative aspect of Christian worship that ensures sincerity, emotional engagement, intentionality, and focus in our adoration of Jehovah. It calls for a lifestyle of continuous worship, integrating not just our moments of prayer or Sunday services but all aspects of our lives. This aspect of worship is not about achieving an emotional high but is about an authentic, deep-seated relationship with God, based on a clear understanding of who He is as revealed in Scripture.

Worshiping in spirit is a challenging yet rewarding endeavor, bringing us into a closer relationship with Jehovah and fulfilling the very purpose for which we were created—to glorify God. Let us aim to be true worshipers, those who worship Jehovah in spirit and truth, recognizing that this is the kind of worshiper the Father seeks.

The Importance of Truth in Worship

Worship is a cornerstone of the Christian faith, a manifestation of our relationship with Jehovah. While worship is an expression of awe, gratitude, and love, the presence of "truth" in worship is not optional but foundational. The necessity of worshiping in "spirit and truth" is directly commanded by Jesus in John 4:23. This paper will expound on the indispensable role that truth plays in worship according to the literal interpretation of Scripture, in line with a conservative, Historical-Grammatical method of interpretation.

The Biblical Definition of "Truth"

In Scripture, "truth" is not a fluid or relative concept but is rooted in the very character of God. Psalm 31:5 refers to Jehovah as the "God of truth." Truth is absolute, unchanging, and eternal, just like Jehovah Himself (Malachi 3:6, Hebrews 13:8). Understanding what truth is, according to Scripture, lays the groundwork for incorporating truth into worship.

The Priority of Scriptural Truth

Jesus stated, "Your word is truth" (John 17:17, ESV). The Scriptures are the supreme authority for defining what is true and what is not. Worship, to be acceptable to God, must align with the truth as revealed in the Bible. This involves the accurate understanding of who God is, what He has done, and how He has revealed Himself to humanity.

Truth in the Content of Worship

The songs, hymns, and spiritual songs that form part of our worship must be scrutinized for their doctrinal accuracy. Singing songs with theologically unsound lyrics is contrary to the principle of worshiping in truth. Paul's exhortation to "Let the word of Christ dwell in you richly, teaching and admonishing one another in all wisdom, singing psalms and hymns and spiritual songs" (Colossians 3:16, ESV), underscores the importance of Scriptural truth as the content of our worship.

The Role of Truth in Prayer

In worship, prayer serves as a direct line of communication with God. It is vital that our prayers are based on Scriptural truths, acknowledging Jehovah for who He truly is and thanking Him for what He has genuinely done. Petitions should be rooted in the promises and teachings of Scripture. Prayers based on falsehoods or misunderstandings about God's nature do not honor Him.

Truth in Preaching and Teaching

The preaching and teaching component of worship services should be deeply rooted in truth. Paul's charge to Timothy was to "preach the word" (2 Timothy 4:2, ESV). Preaching that strays from Scriptural truth is not only ineffective but also dishonoring to Jehovah.

Truth and Personal Integrity

Worshiping in truth is not merely about doctrinal accuracy; it also pertains to personal integrity. Being truthful before Jehovah in our worship means coming before Him as we truly are, without pretense or hypocrisy. The story of Ananias and Sapphira in Acts 5 stands as a stern warning against dishonesty in our worship lives.

Truth and Cultural Sensitivities

In our multi-cultural, pluralistic societies, there is a tendency to dilute the "truth" to make worship more inclusive or less offensive. However, the truth as it stands in Scripture is non-negotiable. While styles of worship may vary culturally, the truth content must remain constant.

The Perils of Ignoring Truth

Ignoring the element of truth in worship can lead to idolatry. When we worship based on false understandings or conceptions about God, we are essentially worshiping a "god" of our own making, not Jehovah as He has revealed Himself in Scripture (Exodus 20:3-5).

Truth as a Protective Barrier

Truth serves as a protective mechanism against false teaching and heresies. In Ephesians 6:14, the "belt of truth" is a part of the spiritual armor of the Christian. This highlights the protective function of truth, even in the context of worship.

Truth is not just a component but the backbone of genuine worship. A worship service devoid of truth is not merely deficient; it is unacceptable to God. From the songs we sing to the prayers we offer, from the sermons we listen to or deliver, to the personal integrity we bring into our worship, truth is the litmus test for each element.

When we align our worship with truth, we align it with God Himself, who is the embodiment of truth. This alignment brings glory to Jehovah and edification to His people. As Jesus emphasized, Jehovah is seeking those who will worship Him in spirit and truth (John 4:23). May we be counted among those true worshipers.

The Convergence of Spirit and Truth

One of the most profound and complex statements by Jesus on the topic of worship appears in His conversation with the Samaritan woman at the well. He declares, "The hour is coming, and is now here, when the true worshipers will worship the Father in spirit and truth, for the Father is seeking such people to worship him" (John 4:23, ESV). This declaration encapsulates the dual essentials of authentic worship: spirit and truth. This paper aims to explore the interrelationship and convergence of these two critical elements in the Christian worship experience.

The Dual Nature of Worship: Spirit and Truth

In John 4:23, Jesus is not presenting two options for worship but is establishing a dual criterion. Worshiping in spirit and truth is not an "either-or" but a "both-and." The two are not independent realms but interdependent aspects that converge to form a holistic worship experience.

The Nature of Spirit in Worship

When Jesus speaks of worshiping in spirit, He is indicating the necessity of genuine, heartfelt, inner worship. It's not about mere outward forms, rituals, or lip service, but about the inner condition of the heart. This aligns with the broader teaching of Scripture that God looks at the heart (1 Samuel 16:7). Worshiping in the spirit involves an earnest, soul-deep relationship with Jehovah, facilitated not by the indwelling of the Holy Spirit—as such a concept is not supported—but by being guided by the Spirit-inspired Word of God.

The Unalterable Standard of Truth

Truth in worship, as we've previously discussed, is about alignment with Scriptural revelation. God's Word is the unchanging standard by which all elements of worship should be judged. This involves not just the content of hymns or sermons but also the attitudes, motivations, and beliefs of the worshiper. Truth is an external standard that exists apart from us but becomes internalized through diligent study and application of Scripture.

The Intersection of Spirit and Truth

When we worship Jehovah, these two aspects of spirit and truth must intersect. Worship that is all "spirit" but lacks truth can lead to emotionalism, subjectivism, and ultimately, heresy. On the other hand, worship that is all "truth" but lacks spirit can lead to empty ritualism, legalism, and a form of godliness that denies its power (2 Timothy 3:5).

The Confluence in Individual Worship

In personal worship, the Christian should engage both the intellect and the emotions. The truth part involves understanding Jehovah, His attributes, and His works as revealed in Scripture. This understanding fuels the "spirit" aspect, resulting in heartfelt prayers, sincere gratitude, and earnest yearning for God's will. The truth of Scripture illuminates the mind, and the spirit responds in genuine worship.

The Convergence in Corporate Worship

In a congregational setting, the role of teaching and preaching is to disseminate the truth of God's Word. This lays the groundwork for the congregation to engage in worship that is both intellectually sound and emotionally genuine. Hymns, prayers, and praises should align with Scriptural truth and, at the same time, enable the worshipers to pour out their spirits before Jehovah.

Practical Implications

1. **Scriptural Literacy**: The more familiar we are with the Scriptures, the more truth-filled our worship will be.
2. **Prayerful Examination**: Before worship, both individually and corporately, prayerful self-examination helps to ensure that one is approaching Jehovah with a true spirit and according to truth.
3. **Vigilance**: The church should be cautious in its selection of songs, teachings, and liturgical elements, ensuring they align with Scriptural truth.
4. **Communal Accountability**: Members of the congregation have a role in maintaining an environment where both spirit and truth are upheld. This is an aspect of the "one another" admonishments seen throughout the New Testament.

Consequences of Dissonance

Failure to integrate spirit and truth in worship is a grave issue. Jehovah desires worshipers who will approach Him on His terms, not on terms we dictate. When spirit and truth are not in harmony, it not only undermines the worship experience but is also an affront to Jehovah, who seeks worshipers who will worship in spirit and truth.

The command to worship Jehovah in spirit and truth is a command to engage Him with both our emotional and intellectual faculties, grounded in the revelation of His Word. This is a high calling, requiring continual self-examination and Scriptural study. However, it's a pursuit worthy of the effort, for it brings us into alignment with Jehovah's will and allows us to worship Him as He has ordained. Therefore, let us be diligent to ensure that our worship of Jehovah is always characterized by this inseparable convergence of spirit and truth.

JOHN 8:32 The Truth Will Set You Free

The Power of Truth

One of the most iconic phrases in Scripture, echoing through millennia, is Jesus' declaration in John 8:32: "And you will know the truth, and the truth will set you free" (ESV). This pivotal assertion, steeped in theological and existential weight, provides an enduring framework for understanding the role of truth in Christian spirituality and freedom. This essay aims to unravel the depths of this statement, its Biblical context, and its implications for the Christian life.

The Immediate Context

To appreciate the gravity of John 8:32, we must understand the immediate context in which Jesus speaks these words. Jesus was engaged in a dialogue with the Jews who had begun to believe in Him. These individuals were still entangled in various traditions and ideologies that were contrary to the revelation of God. Therefore, Jesus' statement serves as a clarion call to discipleship, a discipleship predicated on adherence to His word and the subsequent discovery of truth.

The Concept of Truth

In Christian theology, truth is not merely an abstract concept or philosophical construct; it is grounded in the character of God Himself. God is described as the "God of truth" (Deuteronomy 32:4, Psalm 31:5), and Jesus Himself is "the way, and the truth, and the life" (John 14:6, ESV). The Bible, being the inspired Word of God, is the objective standard for truth, setting the boundaries for belief and practice (2 Timothy 3:16-17).

The Mechanism of Freedom

When Jesus speaks of freedom through truth, He is not advocating for a self-defined liberation, but a freedom defined by God's standards. Biblical freedom is liberation from the bondage of sin (Romans 6:18-22), the crippling weight of legalism (Galatians 5:1), and the darkness of ignorance (Ephesians 4:18). Truth serves as the mechanism that unlocks these various forms of spiritual captivity.

Spiritual Implications of Knowing the Truth

1. **Salvation**: The most immediate implication of knowing the truth is salvation. One must first understand the truth of the Gospel—that mankind is sinful and in need of redemption, and that Jesus is the only Savior—before experiencing the freedom of salvation (Acts 4:12).

2. **Sanctification**: Truth plays an integral role in sanctification. Jesus prays in John 17:17: "Sanctify them in the truth; your word is truth" (ESV). Being transformed into Christlikeness involves aligning one's life with the truth of Scripture.

3. **Moral Clarity**: In a world rife with moral ambiguity, the truth of God's Word offers a clear moral compass. It helps believers discern right from wrong, thereby aiding in making ethical choices that honor Jehovah.

4. **Emotional and Psychological Freedom**: Knowing the truth about oneself, the world, and God can alleviate many emotional and psychological burdens such as guilt, anxiety, and fear.

The Relationship Between Truth and Obedience

True freedom is not just theoretical; it has a practical aspect that involves obedience to the truth. James talks about being "doers of the word, and not hearers only" (James 1:22, ESV). True freedom is experienced through active obedience to the revealed truth in Scripture.

The Corporate Aspect of Truth

Truth is not just an individual pursuit; it has corporate implications as well. The church is described as the "pillar and buttress of the truth" (1 Timothy 3:15, ESV). Therefore, it has the divine mandate to uphold and propagate the truth, which sets people free.

Counterfeits and Dangers

The world offers various counterfeits of truth, usually predicated on human wisdom or ideology. Such paths lead not to freedom but to further bondage. For instance, the secular mantra that "truth is relative" can lead to moral and spiritual chaos.

The Relevance for Contemporary Christians

In our modern world, where "fake news" and misinformation are rampant, the need for truth is more pressing than ever. Christians must be diligent in their pursuit of truth, not just for personal edification but as a tool for evangelism and social influence.

The declaration that "the truth will set you free" encapsulates the liberating power of divine truth. This freedom, however, is not a libertine or self-defined freedom but is grounded in the character and revelation of Jehovah. It is freedom from sin, ignorance, and the moral decay that enslaves the human soul. Therefore, the pursuit of truth is not optional; it is a Christian imperative. In a world shackled by lies and half-truths, may we be relentless in our quest for truth, for in it lies the power for true freedom.

The Chains of Ignorance

Ignorance is not merely a lack of knowledge; in a Biblical sense, it is a spiritual condition that can have devastating consequences. It can lead to sin, suffering, and eternal separation from God. Understanding ignorance from a Biblical standpoint offers insights into the human condition and the need for divine revelation. This essay aims to explore the concept of ignorance in Scripture, its consequences, and the way out through the wisdom and knowledge provided by God.

The Nature of Ignorance in Scripture

Biblical ignorance is not limited to a lack of information or education. It includes an absence of spiritual understanding or the lack of the fear of Jehovah, which is the beginning of wisdom (Proverbs 9:10). Ignorance can stem from various sources: rejecting God's revelation, cultural or religious blindness, or choosing to ignore the available evidence for God's existence and His works. Ignorance of God's law leads to sin, as Hosea 4:6 warns, "My people are destroyed for lack of knowledge; because you have rejected knowledge, I reject you from being a priest to me."

The Chains: Consequences of Ignorance

1. **Spiritual Blindness**: Ignorance often manifests as spiritual blindness. The inability to recognize God's truth makes one susceptible to false doctrines and spiritual deception (2 Corinthians 4:4).
2. **Sin and Separation**: Ignorance leads to sin, and sin leads to separation from God. This is the most disastrous consequence of ignorance (Isaiah 59:2).

3. **Perpetuation of Falsehood**: When ignorance prevails, false doctrines and untruths are easily propagated, leading others astray (Matthew 15:14).

4. **Emotional and Psychological Impact**: Ignorance about the character of God, the love of Christ, and the provisions of grace can lead to anxiety, despair, and even hopelessness.

5. **Stunted Spiritual Growth**: Ignorance hinders one's ability to grow in faith and in the knowledge of God, thereby affecting spiritual maturity (Hebrews 5:12-14).

Breaking the Chains: The Power of Divine Revelation

1. **Word of God**: The Bible is the foundational source of knowledge and wisdom. Through it, we learn about the character of God, the nature of sin, and the means of salvation. Paul affirms in 2 Timothy 3:16-17 that all Scripture is inspired and profitable for teaching, rebuking, correcting, and training in righteousness.

2. **The Spirit-Inspired Word**: The Word of God was inspired by the Holy Spirit and serves as the guide for believers. Though there is no indwelling of the Holy Spirit, we are guided by the Spirit through Scripture (2 Peter 1:21).

3. **Prayer for Wisdom**: Prayer is another avenue through which divine knowledge can be sought. James 1:5 encourages believers to ask God for wisdom, who gives generously to all.

4. **Christian Community**: The Church serves as a collective repository of Scriptural truth. The mutual sharing of insights, experiences, and Scriptural understanding can serve as a bulwark against ignorance (1 Timothy 3:15).

Practical Steps for Overcoming Ignorance

1. **Consistent Bible Study**: Make it a habit to study the Word diligently (Psalm 1:2).

2. **Mentorship**: Seek guidance from seasoned believers who are grounded in the Scriptures (Titus 2:3-5).

3. **Discernment**: Use the Word as the standard for testing all doctrines, teachings, and spiritual experiences (1 John 4:1).

4. **Service and Application**: Apply Scriptural truth in daily life and in serving others. Knowledge becomes powerful when put into practice (James 1:22).

Ignorance is a chain that binds many, leading to sin, spiritual blindness, and eternal loss. However, God in His mercy has provided the means for breaking these chains through His revealed Word and the wisdom that comes from a relationship with Him. To overcome ignorance, therefore, is to submit oneself to the authority and instruction of Scripture, continually seek divine wisdom, and engage in a community that upholds the truth. Only then can one break free from the chains of ignorance and walk in the liberating light of divine knowledge.

Truth as a Path to Freedom

The concept of truth as a path to freedom is deeply embedded in Scripture. The interrelationship between truth and freedom is especially evident in the New Testament, illuminating the transformative power of living in the light of God's truth. This essay aims to explore the Biblical foundation of this theme, its implications for believers, and its significance in the life of the Church.

Defining Truth and Freedom in a Biblical Context

Truth, in the Biblical context, is not merely the absence of falsehood. It is the ultimate reality as embodied in the character of God and revealed in His Word. Jehovah is the "God of truth" (Psalm 31:5), and Jesus Christ declared Himself to be the "way, and the truth, and the life" (John 14:6). Therefore, Biblical truth is immutable, authoritative, and life-giving.

Freedom, on the other hand, is not simply the absence of external constraints but the liberation from sin, death, and spiritual bondage. Paul articulates this beautifully when he says, "For freedom Christ has set us free; stand firm therefore, and do not submit again to a yoke of slavery" (Galatians 5:1).

The Intrinsic Connection: John 8:32

The nexus between truth and freedom is explicitly stated in John 8:32: "and you will know the truth, and the truth will set you free." Here, Jesus underscores the liberating power of truth.

1. **Truth Liberates from Sin**: Sin is the ultimate bondage that enslaves humanity. When we come to know the truth of God's redemptive plan, we are set free from this enslavement (Romans 6:18).

2. **Truth Liberates from Deception**: In a world filled with false ideologies, half-truths, and lies, the truth of God's Word provides the discernment needed to navigate life's complexities (1 John 4:1).

3. **Truth Liberates from Fear**: The knowledge of God's sovereign control and the assurance of His promises liberate believers from fear and anxiety (2 Timothy 1:7).

4. **Truth Liberates from Legalism and Ritualism**: Knowing the truth about the grace of God frees believers from the bondage of legalistic rituals and traditions that cannot save (Galatians 2:16).

The Role of the Word and the Spirit-Inspired Word

The Word of God serves as the foundational repository of truth. Through its pages, believers come to know the nature of God, the story of redemption, and the guidelines for righteous living. Paul stated that "All Scripture is breathed out by God and profitable for teaching, for reproof, for correction, and for training in righteousness" (2 Timothy 3:16). Although the Holy Spirit does not indwell believers, the Spirit-inspired Word serves as a guiding light in the believer's walk.

Practical Steps for Walking in Truth and Freedom

1. **Commit to Diligent Study**: A disciplined approach to studying Scripture is crucial. It equips us to discern truth from error (2 Timothy 2:15).

2. **Apply the Word**: Truth is meant to be applied. Freedom is experienced when we put the Word into practice (James 1:22).

3. **Seek Accountability**: In a community of believers, accountability helps us to stay committed to the truth (Hebrews 10:24-25).

4. **Pray for Wisdom**: Wisdom, the correct application of truth, is a gift from God that we should continually seek through prayer (James 1:5).

5. **Engage in Outreach**: Sharing the truth is integral to experiencing the fullness of the freedom it brings. Evangelism and discipleship are essential Christian duties that impart both truth and freedom (Matthew 28:19-20).

The link between truth and freedom is not merely conceptual but profoundly experiential. When believers embrace the truth of God's Word, they experience unparalleled freedom—freedom from sin, deception, fear, and legalism. This relationship between truth and freedom should motivate every believer to pursue a life rooted in Scriptural truth. As we do so, not only will we experience personal freedom, but we will also become conduits of this freedom to a world in desperate need of both truth and liberation.

The Liberating Message of Jesus

The message of Jesus Christ stands as a cornerstone of hope, redemption, and freedom in the Christian faith. Throughout His earthly ministry, Jesus consistently preached a message that was not only revolutionary for its time but remains universally liberating. This essay will delve into the essence of Jesus' liberating message by examining the key components of His teachings and how they set the captives free, both spiritually and morally.

The Core of the Message: The Kingdom of God

Jesus inaugurated His ministry with a proclamation of the Kingdom of God. In Mark 1:15, He states, "The time is fulfilled, and the Kingdom of God is at hand; repent and believe in the Gospel." Here, Jesus is saying that the ultimate reign of God has come near and that it demands a response—repentance and faith.

1. **Spiritual Liberation**: The Kingdom of God is not just a future reality but a present one. Jesus brings spiritual freedom by offering redemption from sin and its ultimate consequence—eternal separation from God (John 3:16).
2. **Moral Liberation**: Jesus' teaching emphasized moral integrity, not just ritualistic purity. The Kingdom calls for a radical internal transformation (Matthew 5:20).

Freedom from Sin and Death

Central to the liberating message of Jesus is the concept of freedom from sin and death. Through His atoning sacrifice on the cross, He offered a way out of the bondage of sin and the sting of death (Romans 6:23). Paul succinctly says, "For the wages of sin is death, but the free gift of God is eternal life in Christ Jesus our Lord" (Romans 6:23).

The New Covenant: A Relational Perspective

Jesus introduces a New Covenant, ratified with His own blood, that provides a direct relationship between the believer and Jehovah (Matthew 26:28). Unlike the Old Covenant, where law was written on stone tablets, the New Covenant writes the law on human hearts, making obedience a natural outcome of a transformed life (Hebrews 8:10).

Freedom from Legalism and Hypocrisy

The Pharisees were the epitome of religious legalism and hypocrisy in Jesus' time. Christ's message tore down these artificial barriers of self-righteousness (Matthew 23). In contrast, Jesus preached that true righteousness emanates from a transformed heart, not external compliance to religious norms (Matthew 5:21-48).

The Power of Truth

Jesus declared Himself to be the embodiment of Truth (John 14:6). He said, "And you will know the truth, and the truth will set you free" (John 8:32). Here, the liberating nature of truth is underscored. In a world filled with illusions, the truth of Christ's message frees individuals from:

1. **Ignorance**: Knowing the true nature of God.
2. **Fear**: The assurance of God's control and promises.
3. **Deception**: Discernment to navigate false ideologies.

Socio-Economic Liberation

While Jesus' primary mission was spiritual in nature, His teachings have social and economic implications. His denunciation of greed and exploitation and His emphasis on social justice (Luke 6:20-26) laid the foundation for a more equitable society. The early church, inspired by Jesus' teachings, was marked by communal living and sharing of resources (Acts 2:44-45).

Practical Implications for Believers

1. **Embrace the Kingdom**: Living under the Kingdom rule means acknowledging the lordship of Christ in all aspects of life.
2. **Walk in Holiness**: Righteousness is not just a legal status but a lifestyle. Walking in holiness reflects our inner transformation.
3. **Value Community**: The message of Jesus fosters not just individual freedom but communal well-being. We are called to love, support, and uplift one another (1 Corinthians 12:25-27).
4. **Commit to Truth**: Being followers of Jesus means being people of truth, in word and deed. This involves constant engagement with the Scriptures, prayer, and a willingness to correct ourselves when we stray.

The liberating message of Jesus stands as a beacon of hope in a world laden with spiritual, moral, and socio-economic bondage. The Gospel, at its core, is a message of freedom—freedom from sin, freedom from legalism, freedom from fear, and freedom from social injustices. As followers of Christ, we are not just the beneficiaries of this liberation but also its ambassadors. Let us therefore strive to live in the freedom Christ has granted us and extend this freedom to a world in desperate need. This involves a relentless commitment to truth, justice, and a life of holiness, rooted in the unchanging truth of God's Word.

JOHN 17:17 Your Word Is Truth

The Divine Source of Truth

In a world inundated with opinions, philosophies, and ideologies, the question of what is genuinely true becomes more pertinent than ever. In the high priestly prayer of John 17, Jesus invokes a statement of absolute significance: "Sanctify them in the truth; your word is truth" (John 17:17, ESV). This affirmation provides a cornerstone for understanding not only the nature of truth but also its source. This essay will explore the profound theological and practical implications of recognizing God's Word as the ultimate standard of truth.

Context: The High Priestly Prayer

Understanding the background of John 17 helps illuminate the weight of Jesus' statement. Jesus is praying to Jehovah for His disciples right before His crucifixion. He is asking for their sanctification, a process of being set apart for holy use. The means for this sanctification, according to Jesus, is "the truth." Not just any truth, but the truth grounded in God's Word.

The Nature of Divine Truth

1. **Infallible and Inerrant**: The Scriptures declare themselves to be the inspired Word of God (2 Timothy 3:16). Because they come from an infallible God, they are themselves infallible and inerrant.

2. **Complete**: God's Word is comprehensive in its teaching about God's character, human nature, and the plan of redemption. While not exhaustive in every detail, it is wholly sufficient for faith and practice (2 Peter 1:3).

3. **Immutable**: Unlike human understandings, which evolve and sometimes contradict themselves, God's truth is unchanging (Malachi 3:6; Hebrews 13:8).

Theological Implications

1. **Epistemology**: God's Word serves as the ultimate epistemological foundation. Epistemology deals with the study of knowledge—its nature, origin, and limits. For the Christian, God's Word becomes the lens through which all other 'truths' are evaluated.

2. **Sanctification**: Truth has a purifying effect on the believer. Aligning one's life with divine truth leads to holiness and sanctification, as Jesus prayed (John 17:17).

3. **Soteriology**: Truth is also soteriological, meaning it has implications for salvation. Jesus Himself declared that the knowledge of the truth would set people free—free from sin and its eternal consequences (John 8:32).

Distinctions in Truth

1. **Objective vs. Subjective**: The claim that God's Word is truth argues for an objective standard of truth that exists apart from human opinion. Subjective truths may change, but objective truths do not.

2. **Moral vs. Amoral**: While all truth is God's truth, not all truth has moral implications. Mathematical truths, for example, are amoral. However, when we speak of God's Word as truth, we primarily refer to moral and spiritual truths that govern behavior and belief.

Practical Implications for Believers

1. **Discernment**: In a world where 'false gospels' abound, discernment becomes crucial. A commitment to God's Word provides the believer with the tools necessary to sift through falsehood and heresy (1 John 4:1).

2. **Apologetics**: God's Word, being the ultimate source of truth, equips the believer to give a defense for the hope within them (1 Peter 3:15). It acts as a foundation upon which rational arguments for the faith can be built.

3. **Ethical Living**: Recognizing God's Word as the divine source of truth will inherently lead to ethical and upright living. The Bible offers timeless principles for morality, social justice, and personal conduct (Micah 6:8).

4. **Transformation**: The ultimate end of truth is not knowledge but transformation. An engagement with divine truth should result in a life increasingly reflective of Christ (Romans 12:2).

The World's Reaction

It should be noted that the world often resists divine truth because it convicts and challenges (John 3:19). The proclamation of God's Word as the ultimate truth will seldom be met with universal applause. However, the Christian's commitment is not to popularity but to fidelity to God's Word.

The declaration of God's Word as the source of truth, as expressed by Jesus in John 17:17, carries an expansive range of theological and practical implications for the believer. It establishes the Bible as the final authority on matters of belief and practice, and it emphasizes the sanctifying power of truth. The assertion also necessitates a life of obedience, discernment, and defense of the faith, even when faced with societal opposition. Thus, to comprehend and accept God's Word as truth is to be transformed by it, to navigate life through it, and to stand firm upon it as the unshakable foundation for all eternity. Indeed, God's Word is not merely a truth among others; it is the truth—absolute, objective, and eternally reliable.

The Role of Scripture in Spiritual Life

Scripture occupies a pivotal role in the life of a Christian believer, shaping not only their understanding of God but also their entire existential reality. This critical examination delves into the indispensable role of the Bible—comprising the Old and New Testaments—in spiritual growth, sanctification, and a life of discipleship. While society has manifold options for spiritual guidance, the Christian turns to Scripture as the divinely inspired, inerrant, and comprehensive guide for all matters of faith and practice.

The Divine Origin of Scripture

Before discussing its role, it's crucial to emphasize that the Bible is God-breathed (2 Timothy 3:16). Every word comes from God, serving as a conduit of His will, His character, and His expectations from humanity. This makes Scripture the primary channel through which God communicates with us, demonstrating its indispensability in spiritual life.

Theological Foundations from Scripture

1. **Understanding God**: The Scripture reveals who God is—His attributes, His works, His plans, and His will. Through it, we comprehend essential doctrines about the Trinity, Christ's deity and humanity, and the work of redemption.

2. **Human Nature**: The Bible provides a thorough understanding of human nature, revealing man's inherent sinfulness and the need for redemption (Romans 3:23, 6:23).

3. **Eschatology**: Our future hope and what awaits humanity in the eschaton are vividly outlined in Scripture. This shapes how we live today and influences our spiritual state.

Roles in Spiritual Formation and Sanctification

1. **Revelation**: Scripture serves as a vehicle for divine revelation. It is the primary means through which God reveals His will to His people.

2. **Instruction**: The Word of God serves as a manual for Christian living. Principles for moral and ethical conduct are meticulously laid out in passages like the Sermon on the Mount (Matthew 5-7).

3. **Conviction**: Scripture has the power to pierce the human heart and bring about conviction of sin (Hebrews 4:12). This leads to repentance and a deeper commitment to a sanctified life.

4. **Encouragement and Comfort**: During trials and suffering, Scriptures offer comfort and hope. The Psalms are replete with expressions of trust in God during distressing times.

5. **Prayer and Worship**: Scripture guides us in how to approach God in prayer and worship. From the Lord's Prayer (Matthew 6:9-13) to the doxologies in Revelation, Scripture gives form and substance to our worship.

Discipleship and Evangelism

1. **Making Disciples**: Christ's Great Commission (Matthew 28:19-20) makes it clear that discipleship involves teaching all that He has commanded. This is impossible without a thorough engagement with Scripture.

2. **Witnessing**: The Good News is derived from the Bible. Effective witnessing and evangelism are built on a Scriptural foundation. Passages like Romans Road layout the gospel message in a clear, straightforward manner.

3. **Apologetics**: For defending the faith, Scriptures give us the guidelines and content (1 Peter 3:15). It equips the believer to engage effectively in religious discourse and stand firm against ideological attacks.

Ethical and Moral Decision-Making

Scripture is the Christian's compass for moral and ethical decisions. The Ten Commandments, Christ's teachings, and Pauline ethics provide robust frameworks for making choices that honor God.

Counter-Cultural Living

In a world that often stands in stark contrast to Biblical values, Scripture equips the believer for a counter-cultural lifestyle. It empowers Christians to take stands on issues like the sanctity of life, the definition of marriage, and the nature of justice, even when such stands are unpopular.

Practical Implications

1. **Bible Study and Meditation**: Regular engagement with the Word is not an option but a requirement. Through study and meditation, the believer internalizes the divine truths and principles enshrined in Scripture.
2. **Community**: The Christian community serves as a context where Scriptural truths are taught, discussed, and lived out. This is in line with the New Testament pattern of believers devoting themselves to the apostles' teaching (Acts 2:42).
3. **Spiritual Disciplines**: Activities like prayer, fasting, and worship find their basis and direction in Scripture. It informs and enriches these practices, making them meaningful and transformative.

Scripture's role in the spiritual life of a Christian is multifaceted and all-encompassing. It is not just a book to be read but a life-source to be lived out. Its role is not limited to Sundays or quiet times but permeates every aspect of existence. Understanding this compels a commitment to regular study and application of God's Word, not as a religious obligation but as a joyous, life-giving relationship with the God who has revealed Himself therein. Therefore, Scripture remains the constant, unshakeable foundation upon which the believer constructs a life of faith, hope, and love.

Truth as a Means of Sanctification

The concept of sanctification—becoming increasingly set apart for God's purpose and conformed to the likeness of Christ—is a vital part of the Christian journey. One of the essential tools that God employs in our sanctification process is Truth. This essay explores how Truth, as revealed in the Bible, serves as an indispensable means for our sanctification.

The Nature of Truth

Before diving into the mechanisms of sanctification, it is essential to define what Truth means within the biblical framework. Truth in Scripture is not merely an abstract idea or a subjective reality; it is a direct reflection of God's character and His will. Jesus said, "I am the way, and the truth, and the life" (John 14:6, ESV), highlighting that Truth is personified in Him. It also encompasses the teachings and principles outlined in the Scriptures.

The Basis: Jesus Christ as the Truth

As believers, our sanctification is fundamentally tied to our relationship with Jesus Christ. His life, teachings, and sacrifice lay the groundwork for our spiritual growth. It is therefore vital to understand that Truth, for the Christian, is more than a set of ethical guidelines—it is a living, breathing reality rooted in Christ.

Sanctification through the Word of God

Jesus prayed for His disciples, "Sanctify them in the truth; your word is truth" (John 17:17, ESV). This petition reveals the instrumental role of divine Truth in sanctification:

1. **Revelation of God's Will**: God's Word makes known His righteous standards and expectations, providing a framework for holy living (Psalm 119:105).

2. **Exposure and Conviction of Sin**: The Truth revealed in Scripture penetrates the heart, exposing areas of sin that require repentance and transformation (Hebrews 4:12).

3. **Guidance**: The Bible acts as a compass, providing spiritual direction and wisdom in navigating life's complexities (Proverbs 3:5-6).

The Armor of God: The Belt of Truth

Paul, in Ephesians 6:14, refers to the Belt of Truth as a part of the Armor of God. This metaphor illuminates how Truth functions in our spiritual defense system:

1. **Foundation for Other Virtues**: Just as a belt holds other pieces of armor in place, Truth serves as the foundation for other virtues like righteousness, peace, and faith.

2. **Protection Against Deception**: In a world rife with lies and distortions, the Belt of Truth provides a defense against spiritual deception and moral compromise.

Practicing Truth in Everyday Life

1. **Authenticity**: Truthfulness should extend to our interactions and relationships, cultivating an environment of authenticity and trust.

2. **Moral and Ethical Choices**: Making decisions based on biblical Truth ensures that we are aligning ourselves with God's will.

3. **Community and Fellowship**: Truth practiced within the context of a Christian community provides accountability and mutual encouragement in the sanctification process.

Truth as a Catalyst for Spiritual Growth

1. **Personal Examination**: Regular self-examination against the Truth of God's Word leads to a recognition of our shortcomings and areas where growth is needed.
2. **Prayer**: Praying in accordance with Truth aligns our will with God's, opening avenues for sanctification.
3. **Spiritual Disciplines**: Activities such as fasting, prayer, and worship are enriched and guided by the Truth, making them effective tools for spiritual growth.

The Role of the Holy Spirit

While the Holy Spirit does not indwell believers, it's important to recognize that the Spirit-inspired Word of God is the medium through which the sanctifying work happens. The Holy Spirit was involved in the revelation and preservation of Truth (2 Peter 1:21), thus serving as a conduit of sanctification by guiding us through the Word.

Dangers of Relativism

A final point to consider is the danger posed by the cultural trend of relativism, which asserts that truth is subjective. Such a mindset is contrary to the objective, unchanging Truth revealed in Scripture, and adopting it can hinder the sanctification process.

Sanctification is an ongoing process of becoming more like Christ, and Truth serves as a critical instrument in this endeavor. The Scriptures, the life of Christ, the guidance of the Spirit through the Word, and the application of biblical principles in daily living all converge to facilitate the sanctification of the believer. The believer, therefore, must be committed to pursuing, understanding, and applying this Truth as a lifelong disciple of Christ. In doing so, Truth becomes not just a concept but an active, transformative power in the life of the Christian, leading to deeper intimacy with God and a more effective witness in the world.

The Efficacy of God's Word

The concept of the "efficacy" of God's Word involves understanding its power and effectiveness in accomplishing God's purposes, especially in the lives of believers.

The question of how God's Word works—its "efficacy"—is profoundly significant, not just for biblical scholars and theologians, but for every Christian seeking a life transformed by Scripture.

The Inherent Power of God's Word

Firstly, it's vital to acknowledge that the Word of God is not just any book. It's inspired by the Holy Spirit, as affirmed in 2 Timothy 3:16-17 (ESV), "All Scripture is breathed out by God and profitable for teaching, for reproof, for correction, and for training in righteousness, that the man of God may be complete, equipped for every good work." In its divine origin, the Word of God carries inherent power and authority.

The Creating Word

In the beginning, God spoke, and the world came into being (Genesis 1). The spoken Word of God has creative power; it brings things into existence. This same power is evident in God's written Word. When Scripture speaks, things happen: hearts are transformed, minds are renewed, and lives are changed.

Living and Active

Hebrews 4:12 (ESV) declares, "For the word of God is living and active, sharper than any two-edged sword, piercing to the division of soul and of spirit, of joints and of marrow, and discerning the thoughts and intentions of the heart." The Bible is not merely ink on paper but a living and active force. Its words have the capacity to penetrate the human heart, expose sin, and guide people toward righteousness.

Agent of Transformation

The Word serves as a primary tool for sanctification, which refers to the process of becoming more like Christ. As mentioned in John 17:17 (ESV), "Sanctify them in the truth; your word is truth." Through Scripture, believers gain wisdom, are convicted of sin, and learn how to live righteous lives.

Clarity and Understanding

Psalm 119:130 (ESV) states, "The unfolding of your words gives light; it imparts understanding to the simple." The Word provides clarity, offering answers to life's questions and dilemmas. When read with a seeking heart, Scripture can clear up misunderstandings, provide direction, and offer profound wisdom that transcends human intellect.

Conviction and Repentance

One of the most immediate effects of engaging with Scripture is the conviction of sin. The Apostle Peter's sermon in Acts 2, rooted in the prophecies of the Old Testament, led to the deep conviction of his listeners and resulted in mass repentance and conversion. Thus, the Word of God serves as an instrument of conviction, bringing people to a realization of their need for repentance.

Faith Comes from Hearing

Paul declares in Romans 10:17 (ESV), "So faith comes from hearing, and hearing through the word of Christ." The Word of God is instrumental in igniting faith. This implies that engagement with the Scriptures is not a passive act but one that can lead to transformative faith.

As A Weapon

Scripture is depicted as part of the Christian's spiritual armor in Ephesians 6, specifically as the "sword of the Spirit" (Ephesians 6:17, ESV). In spiritual warfare, the Word is both a defensive and offensive weapon, able to counter the lies and temptations of the enemy.

God's Word Never Returns Void

Isaiah 55:11 (ESV) declares, "So shall my word be that goes out from my mouth; it shall not return to me empty, but it shall accomplish that which I purpose, and shall succeed in the thing for which I sent it." God's Word is always effective; it accomplishes the purposes for which it was sent.

Limitations of Human Will

While the Word of God is effective and powerful, it's important to note that human will plays a role in the equation. We are exhorted to "receive with meekness the implanted word, which is able to save your souls" (James 1:21, ESV). Human resistance can limit the transformative potential of Scripture. However, the Word has the power to break down these barriers over time.

The efficacy of God's Word is not a matter of conjecture but a truth substantiated by Scripture itself and witnessed through its transformative power in the lives of countless believers. It is living, active, penetrating, and transformative. The Word of God has the unparalleled power to sanctify, to guide, to convict, and to instill faith. Its impact is not solely for individual benefit but serves to equip the Church collectively for the work of the ministry. The Christian, therefore, ought to be deeply committed to regular interaction with this efficacious Word, confident that it is powerful and purposeful, entirely sufficient for every spiritual need.

JOHN 18:38 What Is Truth

Pilate's Puzzling Question

The interrogation of Jesus by Pontius Pilate in John 18 is one of the most enigmatic and profound interactions in the New Testament. Pilate's question, "What is truth?" (John 18:38, ESV), has captivated theologians, philosophers, and laypersons alike for centuries. What was Pilate asking? Was it a sincere inquiry or a cynical retort? This article seeks to unpack the layers of this question within its historical, cultural, and spiritual contexts and to explore its implications for the Christian believer.

The Context of the Question

Before diving into Pilate's question, we should examine the surrounding context. Jesus is brought to Pilate on charges of blasphemy and claiming to be the King of the Jews. Pilate is attempting to discern the nature of Jesus' kingdom to determine if He is a political threat. When Jesus claims that His kingdom is not of this world and that He came to "bear witness to the truth," Pilate poses his famous question.

Pilate's Skepticism

The prevalent thought in the Roman and Greek world at that time was increasingly skeptical about the notion of absolute truth. Philosophical currents such as Stoicism, Epicureanism, and early forms of Skepticism all had differing views about what constituted truth and whether it could be known. So, Pilate's question could reflect the general skepticism of his era.

Pilate's Position

It's crucial to remember that Pilate was a Roman governor, an official representative of the Roman Empire. He was accustomed to dealing with the harsh realities of politics, power struggles, and manipulative tactics. His primary concern was to maintain order and stability in his jurisdiction. Truth, for him, may have been more about what could be pragmatically applied to maintain that order, rather than an eternal, immovable standard.

The Irony of the Situation

The profound irony here is that Pilate asks about the nature of truth while Truth Himself stands before him. Jesus had earlier declared, "I am the way, and the truth, and the life" (John 14:6, ESV). The very embodiment of Truth was on trial, yet Pilate fails to recognize this.

The Nature of Truth According to Scripture

According to the Bible, truth is not just an abstract concept but a characteristic of God Himself. "The sum of Your word is truth," declares the Psalmist (Psalm 119:160, ESV). God's nature defines truth, and because God is unchanging, truth is also absolute and unchanging. It's crucial to understand that truth, according to the Bible, is not a result of cultural consensus or individual perception but rooted in the character and nature of God.

The Search for Truth

The search for truth should not be a mere intellectual exercise but a transformative endeavor. The Apostle Paul warned Timothy about those who are "always learning and never able to arrive at a knowledge of the truth" (2 Timothy 3:7, ESV). It is not enough to merely acknowledge the truth; one must also act upon it, as James admonishes believers to be "doers of the word, and not hearers only" (James 1:22, ESV).

The Truth that Liberates

Earlier in John's Gospel, Jesus had taught that "the truth will set you free" (John 8:32, ESV). This speaks not only to the intellectual freedom gained by understanding God's truth but also to the spiritual freedom obtained through Christ. Truth is not oppressive; it is liberating because it guides us toward the very purposes for which we were created.

The Consequences of Ignoring Truth

Ignoring or rejecting truth has severe consequences. Paul's letter to the Romans tells us that some "exchanged the truth about God for a lie" (Romans 1:25, ESV). When truth is exchanged for a lie, it leads to a distorted view of reality and, consequently, to moral and spiritual decay.

The Church's Role in Upholding Truth

The Church is called to be the "pillar and buttress of truth" (1 Timothy 3:15, ESV). It is through the Church that God's manifold wisdom is made known (Ephesians 3:10). In a world where the concept of absolute truth is increasingly being questioned or dismissed, the Church has an essential role in upholding and proclaiming the unchanging truth of God's Word.

Pilate's question, "What is truth?" is a haunting one that continues to resonate today. According to Scripture, truth is not merely an abstract concept but a person—Jesus Christ. As believers, understanding this should transform not only our worldview but our very lives. Truth is rooted in the character of God; it is absolute, and it demands our response. Just like Pilate, we find ourselves face to face with Truth, and we must decide whether to accept it or reject it. The decision is crucial because, in the words of Jesus, "whoever is of the truth listens to my voice" (John 18:37, ESV). Hence, our stance on truth is not just a matter of intellectual affirmation but a pivotal issue that has eternal implications.

The Nature of Biblical Truth

The concept of "truth" has been debated, dissected, and discussed across millennia by philosophers, theologians, and scholars. However, the nature of Biblical truth stands as a unique category with particular attributes and implications. This essay aims to elucidate the key aspects of the nature of Biblical truth and its significance for the Christian believer.

Truth as God's Nature

At its core, Biblical truth is inextricably linked with the nature of God Himself. In the book of Numbers, Jehovah is described as a God who is "not man, that he should lie" (Numbers 23:19, ESV). Jehovah's inability to lie is not due to some external moral constraint but is rooted in His very character. Truth, then, is not an abstract concept that God aligns Himself with; rather, He is the very source and foundation of all truth.

Truth as Absolute

One of the most controversial aspects of Biblical truth in our postmodern age is its claim to absoluteness. When Jesus claims, "I am the way, and the truth, and the life" (John 14:6, ESV), He makes a radical, non-negotiable statement about the nature of truth. Contrary to relativistic views that argue for a malleable truth dependent on individual perspectives, Biblical truth posits that there are unchangeable facts which exist independent of human opinion.

Truth as Objective

Connected with its absoluteness is the objectivity of Biblical truth. In a culture that often elevates subjective experiences or feelings as the ultimate authority, the Bible challenges us to measure all things against the objective standard of God's Word. For instance, the Bereans in the book of Acts were commended for verifying Paul's teachings against the Scriptures, not their feelings or experiences (Acts 17:11).

Truth as Revealed

An important aspect of Biblical truth is its revealed nature. We could not know God or His truths through human wisdom or efforts alone. Paul tells us that "in the wisdom of God, the world did not know God through wisdom" (1 Corinthians 1:21, ESV). It was necessary for God to disclose Himself and His truths to us, which He has done supremely in Jesus Christ and authoritatively in the Scriptures.

Truth as Unified

Although the Bible addresses a plethora of topics—historical, moral, spiritual—it does so with a unified voice. While it is true that the Scriptures were penned by multiple authors over centuries, the consistent message and thematic unity point to a single divine Author. The Old and New Testaments are not isolated or contradictory but form a harmonious narrative that reveals God's plan for human history.

Truth as Purposeful

Biblical truth is not given merely for the sake of information but for transformation. James warns against being merely "hearers" of the Word and not "doers" (James 1:22, ESV). The Scriptures are intended to equip believers "for every good work" (2 Timothy 3:16-17, ESV). Hence, the purpose of Biblical truth is not just intellectual ascent but ethical application and spiritual formation.

Truth as Reliable

The reliability of Biblical truth has been attested to by various means, including archaeology, prophecy, and internal consistency. Peter assures us that the prophetic word is "more fully confirmed" and urges us to "pay attention to this as to a lamp shining in a dark place" (2 Peter 1:19, ESV). This reliability makes the Scriptures a sure foundation upon which to base our lives.

Truth as Exclusive

In a pluralistic society that often promotes a "coexist" mentality toward various belief systems, the exclusive claims of Biblical truth are increasingly unpopular. Yet, the Bible itself leaves no room for syncretism. Jesus' claim to be the only way to the Father (John 14:6) and Peter's assertion that "there is salvation in no one else" (Acts 4:12, ESV) make it clear that Biblical truth is not one among many but the only truth that saves and sanctifies.

Truth as Eternally Significant

Finally, the most sobering aspect of Biblical truth is its eternal significance. Our response to God's truth has everlasting consequences. In the grand scope of eternity, Jesus presents only two paths: one that leads to eternal life and another that leads to eternal destruction (Matthew 7:13-14).

Biblical truth is not an abstract or relative concept but a divine revelation with absolute, objective, and eternal dimensions. It is a truth that demands a response—a truth that beckons us to align ourselves with the very nature and character of God. It informs, transforms, and eternally determines the trajectory of human souls. Therefore, understanding and living in light of Biblical truth is not an optional exercise for the believer but a fundamental obligation and the highest privilege.

The Relativism of the World

The prevailing culture often applauds relativism as a sophisticated, tolerant worldview, dismissing the notion of absolute truth as archaic or even oppressive. In this age where "my truth" and "your truth" are phrases that receive nods of approval, it is crucial to delineate the dangers of relativism from a biblical perspective. This essay aims to elaborate on how relativism undermines objective truth, muddles moral reasoning, and even cripples our relationship with God and fellow humans.

Relativism Defined

Relativism is the belief that truth, morality, and reality are not objective but are, instead, subject to individual or cultural interpretation. This philosophy challenges the biblical understanding of truth as absolute, unchanging, and grounded in the very character of Jehovah. Relativism proposes that what might be true or ethical for one person may not be the same for another, thereby dismantling any objective standard of right and wrong.

Relativism vs. Biblical Truth

Scripture presents truth as non-negotiable and fixed. Jesus Christ declared, "I am the way, and the truth, and the life. No one comes to the Father except through me" (John 14:6, ESV). This statement leaves no room for alternative paths to God or varying interpretations of truth. In stark contrast, relativism promotes the idea that many paths can lead to God, directly undermining the exclusive claims of Christianity and even the nature of God as truth.

The Dangers of Moral Relativism

One of the most pernicious effects of relativism is its impact on moral reasoning. The Ten Commandments, the Sermon on the Mount, and numerous other passages offer clear moral guidelines that are meant to be universally applicable. When moral standards become individualized, societal cohesion unravels. The Apostle Paul warned against such moral degradation in his letters, stating that there would be "lovers of self, lovers of money...lovers of pleasure rather than lovers of God" in the last days (2 Timothy 3:2, 4, ESV).

The Confusion of Subjectivity

Relativism embraces subjectivity at the cost of objective reality. In a worldview where experience or emotion become the arbiters of truth, confusion inevitably follows. This stands in direct opposition to Scripture, which offers an objective standard for both individual and communal conduct. The Psalmist celebrated the clarity that God's Word offers, declaring, "Your word is a lamp to my feet and a light to my path" (Psalm 119:105, ESV).

Erosion of Personal Accountability

By rejecting a fixed standard of truth and morality, relativism also erodes the concept of personal accountability. If every individual's actions are right in their own eyes, then the notion of sin loses its meaning. This fundamentally contradicts the biblical narrative, which holds humanity accountable to God's laws and offers redemption through Jesus Christ.

Spiritual Ramifications

Relativism not only undermines moral living but also compromises the spiritual health of believers and non-believers alike. If all beliefs are equally valid, then the uniqueness and necessity of the Gospel message become diluted. Belief in Jesus Christ as the only way for salvation is reduced to just one option among many, thereby negating the urgency and mandate for evangelism.

Counterfeit Tolerance

Relativism often masquerades as tolerance. While Christians are called to love others, this is not synonymous with validating every belief as true. Biblical love involves pointing people to the truth that can set them free (John 8:32), even if that truth is uncomfortable or unpopular.

Eternal Implications

The gravest danger of relativism lies in its eternal implications. By devaluing the truth of God's Word and the exclusive claims of Jesus Christ, relativism risks leading souls away from the narrow path of salvation towards eternal destruction (Matthew 7:13-14). Therefore, combating relativism is not merely an intellectual exercise but a battle for eternal souls.

Relativism stands in stark contrast to the teachings of Scripture, which assert the existence of absolute, objective truth rooted in the character of Jehovah. While the world may celebrate relativism as a form of enlightened thinking, the Christian must remember that this worldview is fundamentally incompatible with biblical principles. The dangers it poses to moral reasoning, spiritual health, and eternal destinies are too significant to be ignored. Hence, believers are called to "destroy arguments and every lofty opinion raised against the knowledge of God, and take every thought captive to obey Christ" (2 Corinthians 10:5, ESV). Given the stakes, nothing less than a full commitment to God's absolute truth will suffice.

The Answer Found in Christ

In a world besieged by questions regarding morality, meaning, and purpose, the Christian conviction is that all the answers are found in Christ Jesus. The Apostle Paul underscores this central idea in Colossians 2:3, stating that in Christ "are hidden all the treasures of wisdom and knowledge" (ESV). This essay aims to elucidate why and how Christ is the epicenter of divine revelation, moral clarity, and eternal hope.

Christ as the Incarnation of Divine Wisdom

Scripture presents Jesus Christ not merely as a great teacher or moral guide but as the very incarnation of God's wisdom. According to the Gospel of John, "In the beginning was the Word, and the Word was with God, and the Word was God" (John 1:1, ESV). Here, the term "Word" (Logos) captures the essence of divine wisdom and reason, incarnate in the person of Christ. He is not just one who points to the truth; He is the Truth.

Christ and Moral Clarity

A world without Christ is a world groping in moral darkness. The Ten Commandments and the law provided the Israelites with a framework for ethical living, but they could not fully embody or fulfill that law. Jesus Christ, by His perfect life and sacrificial death, not only fulfilled the law but also provided the ultimate exemplar of a morally virtuous life. He epitomized love, compassion, humility, and integrity, demonstrating how to live out God's moral imperatives in a fallen world.

Christ as the Fulfillment of Prophecy

Jesus is not just a random figure who appears abruptly in human history. He is the anticipated Messiah, the focal point of numerous Old Testament prophecies. From the promise of the seed of the woman who would crush the serpent's head (Genesis 3:15) to the suffering servant of Isaiah 53, Jesus Christ completes the narrative arc of Scripture, serving as the key to understanding its overarching message.

The Solace of Christ in Suffering

The problem of human suffering has often been a stumbling block for many. While God allows suffering, the Christian finds solace in the fact that Jesus Christ entered into our suffering. In Him, we have a high priest who can sympathize with our weaknesses and offer comfort in our trials (Hebrews 4:15). Christ's suffering on the cross is the profound solution to the problem of pain, displaying God's righteousness while making a way for our redemption.

Christ and Eternal Life

One of the most potent longings of the human soul is the yearning for eternal life. In Jesus Christ, this deep-seated desire finds its fulfillment. "For God so loved the world, that he gave his only Son, that whoever believes in him should not perish but have eternal life" (John 3:16, ESV). The resurrection of Jesus Christ substantiates this promise, ensuring that those who are in Christ will share in His victory over death.

Christ as the Means of Reconciliation

Humanity's greatest need is reconciliation with a holy God. This reconciliation could not be achieved by human efforts or moral striving but only through the atoning work of Jesus Christ on the cross. He satisfied the righteous demands of a holy God, enabling those who put their faith in Him to be declared righteous (Romans 5:1).

Christ as the Fountain of Living Water

In a world parched by spiritual thirst, Jesus offers Himself as the fountain of living water (John 4:14). Those who partake of Him will never thirst again. He fulfills the deepest human needs and desires, which cannot be satisfied by worldly pleasures or pursuits.

Christ and the Call to Discipleship

Finally, the answers found in Christ are not meant merely for personal edification but for transformational discipleship. The Apostle Paul summed up the Christian journey as becoming "conformed to the image of his Son" (Romans 8:29, ESV).

Believers are called to be imitators of Christ, impacting the world through godly living and the proclamation of the Gospel.

Christ is the hub of divine wisdom, moral clarity, and eternal hope. He is the answer to the philosophical, moral, and existential questions that plague the human mind. Moreover, He is the solution to the problem of sin and separation from God, offering Himself as the way, the truth, and the life (John 14:6, ESV). The answers found in Christ are comprehensive, satisfying both the intellect and the soul, while providing a robust framework for ethical living and a vibrant relationship with God. Far from being just one religious figure among many, Christ is the unique and unparalleled answer to humanity's deepest questions and longings. Therefore, as Christians, we are called to "grow in the grace and knowledge of our Lord and Savior Jesus Christ. To him be the glory both now and to the day of eternity. Amen" (2 Peter 3:18, ESV).

ROMANS 1:18 Unrighteous Men Who Suppress the Truth

The Act of Suppressing Truth

The apostle Paul's letter to the Romans is a foundational text that lays out the gospel of Jesus Christ and its implications for humanity. One of the pivotal verses in this epistle is Romans 1:18, which reads: "For the wrath of God is revealed from heaven against all ungodliness and unrighteousness of men, who by their unrighteousness suppress the truth" (ESV). This verse forms the basis for an examination of the human tendency to suppress the truth, the reasons behind this suppression, and its catastrophic consequences.

The Concept of Suppression

The Greek term translated as "suppress" in this verse is *katechō*, which means to hold down or restrain. It implies a deliberate act of holding back or obstructing the truth from having its effect. This suppression is neither passive nor accidental but is an active rebellion against the moral and spiritual reality revealed by God.

Why Do People Suppress the Truth?

The core issue is not that people lack exposure to truth but that they choose to ignore or belittle it. Paul identifies ungodliness and unrighteousness as the root causes of this suppression. People suppress the truth about God's existence, righteousness, and moral law to maintain a lifestyle that is contrary to His will.

1. **Pride**: Many times, the suppression of truth can be traced back to human pride. The fallen human nature resents the idea of being subject to a Higher Power.
2. **Love of Sin**: Some people suppress the truth because acknowledging it would necessitate moral change, which they are not willing to make.
3. **Intellectual Convenience**: For some, dismissing the truths of Christianity is more intellectually comfortable than engaging with them, as this allows them to adhere to worldviews that are simpler but less accurate.
4. **Fear of Social Consequences**: In some cases, the truth is suppressed due to fear of ridicule, social ostracization, or other types of persecution.

The Wrath of God

The suppression of truth is not a matter to be taken lightly; it invokes the wrath of God. Paul is clear that this wrath is "revealed from heaven," signifying that it is divine, just, and universal. It is against all forms of "ungodliness and unrighteousness," encompassing every action, thought, or belief that contradicts God's moral law.

The Role of Natural Revelation

Even if one has not been exposed to the Scriptures or the message of Jesus Christ, Paul argues in Romans 1 that the natural world itself bears witness to the truth of God's existence and attributes. Suppressing this truth, therefore, is without excuse.

Suppression vs. Ignorance

It is crucial to distinguish between those who suppress the truth and those who are ignorant of it. While suppression involves a willful rebellion against known truth, ignorance is a lack of knowledge. However, Paul's argument is that humanity's problem is not ignorance but willful suppression.

The Consequences of Suppressing Truth

The act of suppressing the truth has both temporal and eternal consequences.

1. **Temporal Consequences**: On a societal level, suppression of truth leads to moral relativism, broken relationships, and a plethora of social evils. On a personal level, it leads to a hardened heart and a seared conscience.

2. **Eternal Consequences**: The most severe consequence is eternal separation from God. The suppression of truth is a rejection of the only means of salvation—faith in Jesus Christ.

The Antidote to Suppression

The only solution to this suppression is the Gospel of Jesus Christ. It is the power of God for salvation to everyone who believes (Romans 1:16). The Gospel shines light on the dark corners of human deception, offering a way of reconciliation with God.

Romans 1:18 is a solemn reminder of the human propensity to suppress the truth of God for the sake of unrighteous living. This suppression is a grievous sin that incurs God's just wrath and leads to both temporal and eternal destruction. Yet, the hope of the Gospel stands as the ultimate antidote to this suppression. Through faith in Jesus Christ, individuals can be freed from the bondage of suppression and experience the transformative power of God's truth. As believers, it is our responsibility to proclaim this truth boldly, confronting the culture of suppression and pointing people toward the liberating message of the Gospel.

Consequences of Unrighteousness

The concept of unrighteousness features prominently in the Scriptures, underscoring its incompatibility with the holiness and purity of God. Unrighteousness is essentially a departure from the moral and ethical standards that Jehovah has established for His creation. While grace and forgiveness through Jesus Christ are always available, it's crucial to acknowledge that unrighteousness is not without its consequences—both temporal and eternal.

Defining Unrighteousness

Unrighteousness is the state of being out of alignment with God's moral and ethical standards as revealed in the Scriptures. It includes actions, thoughts, and attitudes that are contrary to God's law. Paul succinctly sums up unrighteousness as a suppression of truth for the sake of living a life contrary to God's will (Romans 1:18).

Temporal Consequences of Unrighteousness

1. **Broken Relationships**: Unrighteousness has an immediate impact on human relationships. For example, deceit breaks trust, and malice can turn friends into enemies.

2. **Spiritual Dullness**: A life of unrighteousness often leads to spiritual dullness, where the voice of conscience becomes increasingly faint, and the discernment of spiritual matters diminishes.

3. **Physical Repercussions**: Some acts of unrighteousness, like gluttony or sexual immorality, may have direct physical consequences such as illness or disease.

4. **Social Disintegration**: On a societal level, unrighteousness can result in the breakdown of social order. Corruption, violence, and dishonesty, when pervasive, can lead to societal decay.

5. **Inescapable Natural Consequences**: Certain acts of unrighteousness have inherent repercussions. For example, theft may result in imprisonment, or lying can lead to loss of reputation.

Eternal Consequences of Unrighteousness

1. **Separation from God**: The ultimate consequence of unrighteousness is eternal separation from God. God's holiness demands that sin be dealt with, and His justice requires a penalty for unrighteousness.

2. **Eternal Destruction**: The Scriptures affirm that unrighteousness will lead to eternal destruction, as opposed to eternal torment (2 Thessalonians 1:9). This is a state of being forever cut off from the goodness and grace of God.
3. **Loss of Heavenly Rewards**: Even for believers, unrighteousness can result in the loss of rewards in the heavenly realm (1 Corinthians 3:14-15). Though they may be saved, their works of unrighteousness are burned up, representing a loss of potential eternal reward.

The Divine Element: God's Wrath

While God is loving and merciful, His wrath against unrighteousness is a reality we must not ignore. This wrath is not arbitrary but is a manifestation of His justice. The "wrath of God is revealed from heaven against all ungodliness and unrighteousness of men" (Romans 1:18, ESV).

The Role of Repentance

Repentance is the turning away from sin and unrighteousness and turning toward God. It is more than just feeling sorry for sin; it involves a change of heart and action. Repentance is essential for receiving God's forgiveness and escaping the consequences of unrighteousness.

The Hope in Christ

While the consequences of unrighteousness are severe, the Scriptures offer hope through Jesus Christ. His sacrificial death on the cross provides the means for humanity to be justified before God, turning unrighteousness into righteousness for those who believe (Romans 5:1).

Role of the Church

The Church plays an essential role in teaching and guiding people away from unrighteousness. Through Scriptural teaching, discipleship, and community, the Church helps believers grow in righteousness.

The consequences of unrighteousness are far-reaching, affecting our temporal lives on earth and our eternal destiny. The Scriptures are unambiguous about the severe repercussions of a life lived in rebellion against God's moral law. However, the grace available through Jesus Christ offers a way out of these dire consequences. It allows those who believe and repent to be reconciled to God, experiencing His love, grace, and eternal blessings. The stark reality of the consequences of unrighteousness should motivate us not only to live holy lives but also to proclaim the truth of the

Gospel with urgency and conviction, directing others toward the redeeming work of Christ.

The Role of Human Rebellion

Human rebellion has been a prominent theme in Scriptural narratives since the early chapters of Genesis. Despite God's clear directives and loving provision, humanity has time and again opted for disobedience, thereby severing its communion with Jehovah. Understanding the role of human rebellion is vital for interpreting the course of human history, the individual's spiritual condition, and the comprehensive plan of redemption.

The Genesis of Rebellion: The Fall

To fully grasp the essence of human rebellion, one needs to delve into the account of Adam and Eve in the Garden of Eden. Their choice to disobey God's command not to eat from the tree of the knowledge of good and evil marked the inception of human rebellion (Genesis 3). This was not merely an act of disobedience; it was an assertion of human independence, implying that man could decide what is good or evil without reference to God. It was, at its core, an act of dethroning God and enthroning oneself.

The Ripple Effects of Rebellion

The rebellion in Eden had both immediate and long-term effects:

1. **Spiritual Death**: The spiritual death that Adam and Eve experienced was an immediate consequence of their rebellion, severing their intimate fellowship with God.

2. **Sin Nature**: This rebellion introduced a sin nature into humanity, passed down from generation to generation. This nature inclines human beings toward disobedience and rebellion against God's authority.

3. **Suffering and Pain**: Rebellion against God is essentially a rebellion against the very source of goodness and life. As a result, human suffering can be seen as an indirect outcome of this rebellion. God didn't design suffering but allows it to demonstrate the inherent flaws in human independence from His sovereignty.

Rebellion in History

Human history is fraught with examples of rebellion against God, from the Tower of Babel to the Israelites' recurrent disobedience in the Old Testament. Even after the advent of Christ, the New Testament writings highlight human rebellion as an ongoing problem, addressed by the apostolic directives for obedience and submission to God's Word.

Theological Implications of Rebellion

1. **Total Depravity**: Although some Christians reject the notion of total depravity in Calvinistic terms, the Scriptures affirm that all of humanity is corrupt and inclined toward rebellion (Romans 3:23).
2. **God's Sovereignty**: Human rebellion has not derailed God's ultimate plans. Jehovah remains sovereign, often using even acts of rebellion to further His divine plans (Joseph's brothers, Pharaoh).
3. **Divine Judgment**: God's righteousness necessitates that rebellion be met with divine judgment. However, this judgment is not eternal torment but eternal destruction, a state of being cut off from God's presence.

The Redemptive Response to Rebellion

The most profound answer to human rebellion is the redemption provided through Jesus Christ. His life, death, and resurrection offer humanity a way to be reconciled to God, moving from a state of rebellion to a state of submission and obedience (Romans 5:10).

1. **Repentance**: The first step in breaking free from rebellion is repentance, a turning away from sin and a turning toward God (Acts 3:19).
2. **Faith in Christ**: Trusting in the finished work of Christ on the cross brings forgiveness and justification, transforming the rebel into a child of God (Ephesians 2:8-9).
3. **Living by the Spirit-inspired Word**: Christians don't have an indwelling of the Holy Spirit but are guided by the Spirit-inspired Word of God, which equips them for a life of obedience (2 Timothy 3:16-17).

Human rebellion is a pervasive, destructive force that underlines the fallen condition of mankind. It has marred our relationship with Jehovah, instigated human suffering, and incurred divine wrath. Nevertheless, God in His infinite wisdom has allowed human rebellion to exist, using it to demonstrate the inherent flaws in human independence and to unfold His glorious plan of redemption. The Scripture offers a way out of this rebellion through repentance and faith in Jesus Christ, directing humanity back to a path of righteousness and obedience. Therefore, understanding the role of human rebellion serves not just as a cautionary tale but also as a beckoning toward God's grace and redemption, urging us to live lives aligned with His eternal truth.

Divine Wrath and Truth Suppressed

Understanding the intersection of divine wrath and the suppression of truth is vital for interpreting the essence of human depravity and God's righteous response. It also reveals the inherent danger in rejecting or modifying God's revelation, both in the form of nature and Scripture. Romans 1:18 states, "For the wrath of God is revealed from heaven against all ungodliness and unrighteousness of men, who by their unrighteousness suppress the truth."

The Wrath of God: A Necessary Expression of Divine Justice

The notion of God's wrath is often misunderstood or deliberately ignored in contemporary discussions about God's character. However, Scripture makes it clear that divine wrath is not a human-like emotional outburst but a consistent and righteous reaction to ungodliness and unrighteousness. The suppression of truth is an affront to God's holy nature and a violation of His moral law, thereby eliciting His righteous wrath. While God is love, His love does not negate His holiness and justice. God's love and wrath are not mutually exclusive; rather, they are two sides of the same coin of His complex, unfathomable nature.

The Act of Suppressing Truth

The apostle Paul states that unrighteous humans suppress the truth. This suppression manifests in various ways:

1. **Denial of General Revelation**: The refusal to acknowledge God as Creator, despite the evidence in the natural world, is a form of suppressing the truth (Romans 1:19-20).

2. **Ignoring or Twisting Scripture**: Rejecting the divine inspiration and authority of the Bible or distorting its teachings to suit human preferences is another form of suppression (2 Peter 3:16).

3. **Idolatry**: Creating gods in our own image or elevating created things above the Creator is a flagrant suppression of the truth (Romans 1:21-23).

4. **Moral Relativism**: Asserting that moral truth is subjective and thereby rejecting the objective moral standards revealed in Scripture is another aspect of this suppression.

Consequences of Suppressing the Truth

1. **Darkened Understanding**: When truth is suppressed, the mind becomes darkened, and spiritual discernment diminishes (Ephesians 4:18).

2. **Hardening of the Heart**: Continued suppression of truth leads to a hardened heart, making one increasingly resistant to God's calling and correction (Hebrews 3:13).

3. **Divine Judgment**: God's wrath is ultimately expressed in divine judgment. In line with the objective Historical-Grammatical method of interpretation and a literal translation philosophy, it must be understood that this judgment is not eternal torment but eternal destruction, a state of being cut off from God's presence.

4. **Perversion and Decay**: The social and moral fabric of society decays when truth is suppressed. This decay manifests as widespread immorality, corruption, and ultimately, societal breakdown.

Divine Purpose in Allowing Truth Suppression

While God didn't design humanity's suppression of truth or the resulting suffering, He allows it as an object lesson demonstrating the futility and consequences of human independence from His sovereignty. Through the sad spectacle of truth suppression, humanity sees the devastating outcomes of straying from God's ordained path.

The Way Out: The Gospel of Jesus Christ

Despite the grim reality of divine wrath and truth suppression, there's hope through the Gospel of Jesus Christ. Acceptance of this Gospel and its inherent truths offers:

1. **Forgiveness and Justification**: Through faith in Jesus, one is forgiven and justified, escaping the wrath of God (Romans 5:9).

2. **Renewal of the Mind**: The Spirit-inspired Word of God has the power to renew the mind, correcting false beliefs and illuminating truth (Romans 12:2).

3. **Empowerment for Righteous Living**: While Christians are not indwelt by the Holy Spirit, they are equipped for righteous living through the Spirit-inspired Word of God (2 Timothy 3:16).

The suppression of truth is a significant and dangerous act that incurs divine wrath. Yet, God's wrath is not an arbitrary act of cruelty but a necessary response to the violation of His moral order. While the consequences of suppressing truth are dire, God's plan of redemption provides a way out, inviting humanity to abandon its futile rebellion and embrace His revealed truths. This transition from suppressing truth to embracing it not only secures one's eternal destiny but also realigns one's life with God's perfect will, thereby circumventing the wrath that is justly due. In this sense, the recognition and acceptance of divine truth serve as both a safeguard against divine wrath and a pathway to a life of fulfilled purpose and everlasting joy.

2 CORINTHIANS 4:2 Not Adulterating the Word of God by Making the Truth Manifest

The Integrity of the Gospel Message

In 2 Corinthians 4:2, Paul boldly declares, "But we have renounced disgraceful, underhanded ways. We refuse to practice cunning or to tamper with God's word, but by the open statement of the truth we would commend ourselves to everyone's conscience in the sight of God." This verse encapsulates a principle foundational to the Christian faith: the integrity of the Gospel message. The clarity, purity, and completeness of the Gospel are central to its transformative power, and thus preserving its integrity is of paramount importance.

The Reality of Adulterating the Word

Adulterating the Word of God occurs in various ways, including:

1. **Adding to Scripture**: Incorporating non-biblical teachings or practices into Christian doctrine is a form of adulteration (Revelation 22:18).

2. **Subtracting from Scripture**: Ignoring or deliberately omitting portions of Scripture that are unpopular or challenging is another form of tampering (Deuteronomy 4:2).

3. **Twisting Scripture**: Taking verses out of context to support a preconceived idea or agenda is a grievous act that undermines the integrity of the Gospel (2 Peter 3:16).

4. **Syncretism**: Blending Christian teachings with other religious or cultural practices also adulterates the purity of the Gospel.

The Gravity of the Act

To adulterate the Word of God is not just a doctrinal error but a moral failing with profound implications:

1. **Erosion of Authority**: Tampering with Scripture undermines its divine authority, leading people away from the truth it contains.

2. **Misguidance of Souls**: An adulterated Gospel cannot lead people to true salvation, endangering their eternal state.
3. **Dishonoring God**: The act essentially calls into question God's wisdom in revealing His will and plans through Scripture.

The Open Statement of Truth

Paul emphasizes that rather than adulterating the Word, the apostolic mission focused on "the open statement of the truth." This phrase denotes complete transparency and fidelity to the revealed will of God:

1. **Sound Doctrine**: The apostles went to great lengths to ensure their teachings accurately represented God's Word, as should any minister of the Gospel.
2. **Ethical Consistency**: Integrity in handling God's Word should be accompanied by moral integrity in life, as the two are interlinked.
3. **Accountability to God and Man**: The truthful handling of the Word should be done with full awareness of accountability to God and the Christian community.

The Role of Conscience

Paul states that this approach would "commend ourselves to everyone's conscience in the sight of God." Here, the conscience serves as the inner moral compass, bearing witness to the truthfulness and integrity of the messenger and the message. The Christian minister's life should be an open book, with nothing to hide, precisely because the truth he upholds is manifestly seen in his character and conduct.

Avoiding Cunning and Craftiness

Paul renounces "cunning" and "underhanded ways," which are methods some might employ to win converts or gain approval. It is a strong warning against using manipulative or deceptive tactics in the propagation of the Gospel. Doing so not only damages one's credibility but also detracts from the Gospel's power to save and sanctify.

Consequences of Adulteration

1. **Loss of Divine Favor**: One who tampers with the Word of God is working against God's purposes and thus risks losing His favor.

2. **Destruction, Not Eternal Torment**: Those who perpetually distort the Word will ultimately face God's judgment, culminating in eternal destruction rather than eternal torment.

The Way Forward

Maintaining the integrity of the Gospel demands constant vigilance and a steadfast commitment to scriptural accuracy. Personal biases, popular trends, or even well-intentioned attempts to make the Gospel more "accessible" should not divert us from this aim. The Spirit-inspired Word of God is our guide and should be consulted regularly to ensure fidelity to the divine message.

Paul's words in 2 Corinthians 4:2 serve as both an exhortation and a caution for those handling the Word of God. The integrity of the Gospel is of supreme importance, as it directly impacts the efficacy of the Christian message and the eternal destinies of souls. Through a committed and transparent approach, rooted in the unadulterated Word of God, ministers and believers alike can uphold the Gospel's integrity, thereby honoring God and effectively ministering to people. This stands as a high calling for every Christian, a charge that demands both our attention and our unwavering dedication.

The Danger of Distorting God's Word

The task of interpreting and communicating God's Word is an immensely significant endeavor with eternal ramifications. Given the gravity of what's at stake, it's critical to address the dangers associated with distorting the Word of God. Distortion can happen intentionally or unintentionally, and in either case, the results are damaging to both the individual and the community of believers. This paper aims to delve into the theological and practical implications of distorting God's Word, and why it should be vehemently avoided.

Biblical Admonitions Against Distortion

Scripture itself contains stern warnings against altering God's Word. Paul warns Timothy of a time when people will not put up with "sound doctrine," choosing instead to surround themselves with teachers who say what their itching ears want to hear (2 Timothy 4:3). In his letter to the Galatians, Paul goes so far as to pronounce an anathema—eternal condemnation—on anyone who preaches a gospel other than the one he had preached (Galatians 1:8-9).

Forms of Distortion

1. **Misinterpretation**: One form of distortion occurs when individuals take passages out of context or assign to them meanings not intended by the original authors. This often happens when people employ eisegesis—reading one's own thoughts into the text—rather than exegesis—drawing out the original meaning of the text.

2. **Selective Emphasis**: Another form of distortion arises when individuals unduly focus on certain passages to the exclusion of others, creating an imbalanced theology. This often results in "pet doctrines" that overlook the full counsel of God.

3. **Extrabiblical Ideas**: Incorporating thoughts, ideas, or philosophies from outside of the Bible into Christian doctrine also constitutes a form of distortion. This syncretism undermines the sufficiency of Scripture.

Theological Implications

1. **Compromised Doctrine**: Distorting God's Word invariably leads to compromised doctrine, which in turn affects the understanding of God, Christ, salvation, and other core Christian beliefs.

2. **Loss of Divine Guidance**: If God's Word is distorted, then the guidance it provides for daily living is compromised. This can lead to sinful behavior and poor decision-making.

3. **Misrepresentation of God**: A distorted message creates a false image of God, which can deter people from coming into a right relationship with Him.

Practical Implications

1. **Diluted Witness**: If the church tolerates or propagates distorted doctrine, its witness to the world becomes diluted. The authenticity and potency of the Gospel message are compromised, rendering evangelistic efforts ineffective.

2. **Divisiveness**: Distortion leads to doctrinal disagreements and divisions within the body of Christ. This impacts the church's ability to function as a unified entity.

3. **Endangering Souls**: Perhaps the most severe implication is the potential eternal loss of souls. A distorted message cannot lead people to the true saving knowledge of Jesus Christ, thereby putting them on a path to eternal destruction, not eternal torment.

The Consequences and Judgment

1. **Loss of Rewards**: Scripture indicates that teachers will be judged more strictly (James 3:1). Those who distort God's Word may lose heavenly rewards, even if they themselves are saved.
2. **Divine Wrath**: Romans 1:18 speaks of the wrath of God being revealed against all who suppress the truth. This could manifest in various ways, both in this life and in the afterlife.

The Antidote

1. **Sound Exegesis**: Employing the objective Historical-Grammatical method of interpretation allows for the extraction of the intended meaning of Scripture, thereby minimizing the risk of distortion.
2. **Accountability**: Christian leaders must hold each other accountable for maintaining doctrinal purity. A plurality of elders or similar church leadership structures can serve as a check against possible distortions.
3. **Diligence and Discernment**: Constant vigilance is required to ensure that one's understanding and teaching remain in alignment with Scripture. This includes a commitment to ongoing biblical studies and an openness to correction.

Distorting God's Word is a dangerous act with profound theological and practical implications. Such distortion not only compromises the core tenets of the Christian faith but also has devastating consequences for the spiritual well-being of individuals and the collective witness of the church. Given these potential outcomes, upholding the integrity of God's Word should be a paramount concern for all believers. It requires a rigorous commitment to sound exegetical practices, mutual accountability, and a continuous pursuit of spiritual discernment. By heeding these principles, we honor God, protect His flock, and preserve the transformative power of His Gospel message.

Manifesting Truth in Ministry

In an age where subjectivity often usurps objectivity and emotions often replace truth, the need for manifesting truth in Christian ministry is more imperative than ever. Scripture makes it abundantly clear that truth is not a peripheral matter; it is the core of God's revelation to humanity. Thus, how truth is managed and manifested within ministry has significant implications for both the individual Christian and the collective Body of Christ. This discussion aims to explore the biblical framework for manifesting truth in ministry, its theological implications, and practical steps to integrate it.

The Biblical Mandate

Paul's second letter to the Corinthians captures the essence of manifesting truth in ministry. He declares, "We refuse to practice cunning or to tamper with God's word, but by the open statement of the truth we would commend ourselves to everyone's conscience in the sight of God" (2 Corinthians 4:2, ESV). The apostle emphasizes integrity and openness, denouncing any form of deceitful practices.

Key Components of Manifesting Truth

1. **Unaltered Message**: Any ministry must begin with the accurate presentation of God's Word. Adulterating God's Word is to commit the gravest of errors, for it distorts the very source of Truth (Proverbs 30:5-6).

2. **Transparent Leadership**: Those in positions of ministry must be transparent, displaying a life that is congruent with the truth they proclaim. Transparency in ministry does not mean airing one's shortcomings publicly, but rather walking in integrity and being open to accountability.

3. **Informed Congregation**: Church members need to be well-versed in Scripture so that they can discern truth from error (Acts 17:11). An ignorant congregation is susceptible to deceit and manipulation.

Theological Implications

1. **Holiness and Sanctification**: Jesus prayed, "Sanctify them in the truth; your word is truth" (John 17:17, ESV). The truth has the power to sanctify, setting individuals apart for God's holy purposes.

2. **Unity**: Adherence to the truth is key to maintaining unity within the church (Ephesians 4:13-15). A common commitment to the truth helps prevent divisions and fosters spiritual growth.

3. **Witness to the World**: The integrity of the Christian witness is upheld when ministry is carried out in truth. Jesus said, "You are the light of the world" (Matthew 5:14, ESV); light is most effective when it is untainted and pure.

Practical Implications

1. **Discipleship Programs**: Discipleship should include intensive Bible study and application. This will not only enhance personal spiritual growth but will also enable believers to contend for the faith (Jude 3).

2. **Accountability Structures**: Implementing an accountability structure can help maintain the integrity of the ministry. This should include financial transparency, checks and balances in leadership, and regular doctrinal reviews.

3. **Community Engagement**: Engaging with the community must be carried out in truth and love. Whether it's social work, evangelism, or inter-faith dialogues, the stand on truth must never be compromised for the sake of peace or acceptance.

4. **Pulpit Ministry**: Preaching must be expository and doctrinally sound, giving due regard to the historical-grammatical context of Scripture. Any deviation from this compromises the integrity of the pulpit.

Potential Pitfalls and Remedies

1. **Popularity over Truth**: The temptation to make the message more palatable to attract larger crowds is a real danger. This is to be avoided at all costs. The objective is not popularity, but faithfulness to God's Word.

2. **Cultural Accommodation**: The urge to adapt the message to suit cultural norms must be resisted. While culture can be engaged, truth must never be compromised (Romans 12:2).

3. **Personal Biases**: Allowing personal opinions and biases to influence the interpretation and preaching of Scripture is another potential pitfall. The antidote is to rigorously employ a sound hermeneutical approach to Scripture.

Manifesting truth in ministry is neither optional nor negotiable; it is a scriptural mandate. It demands a high level of integrity in message delivery, leadership conduct, and congregation involvement. Truth is central to God's redemptive plan for humanity and therefore, must be treated with the utmost respect and diligence. While challenges exist, remaining faithful to the truth ensures a ministry that is both pleasing to God and beneficial to His people. Such a commitment not only affects the spiritual health of the individual Christian but also has a far-reaching impact on the collective witness of the Church to the world. It is a rigorous but rewarding journey, and it is the only pathway that leads to the glorification of God in ministry.

The Accountability of Spiritual Leaders

Accountability is not just a societal norm but a biblical principle that carries significant weight in the Christian community, especially when it concerns spiritual leaders. The charge to shepherd God's flock is no light matter and comes with immense responsibility and accountability to both God and the church community. This essay will delve into the nature, theological underpinnings, and practical implications of the accountability of spiritual leaders, guided by the lens of the Scriptures.

The Nature of Accountability for Spiritual Leaders

1. **Accountability to God**: At the core, every spiritual leader must remember that they are accountable to God Himself. The Apostle Paul admonished Timothy to "preach the word; be ready in season and out of season; reprove, rebuke, and exhort, with complete patience and teaching" (2 Timothy 4:2, ESV). Ultimately, it is before the judgment seat of Christ that a spiritual leader's stewardship will be evaluated (Romans 14:12).

2. **Accountability to Scripture**: Spiritual leaders are also accountable to the truth of God's Word. They are charged with dividing the Word rightly and are held to a stricter judgment for how they handle it (James 3:1).

3. **Accountability to the Congregation**: Being a spiritual leader is a relational role. Leaders are given the duty to watch over souls, and they must give an account for this stewardship (Hebrews 13:17).

Theological Foundations for Accountability

1. **Sovereignty of God**: The Scriptures affirm that all authority comes from God (Romans 13:1). As such, spiritual leaders are essentially stewards of God's authority, and they must exercise it in a way that honors Him.

2. **Sanctity of the Church**: Christ loved the church and gave Himself for it (Ephesians 5:25). If the church is important enough to warrant Christ's sacrificial death, then surely its leaders must be held to a high standard of accountability.

3. **Doctrine of Sin**: The ever-present reality of sin means that spiritual leaders are susceptible to moral failings. An accountability structure acts as a protective measure (1 Corinthians 10:12).

Practical Implications for Accountability

1. **Transparency**: This involves being honest in financial dealings, maintaining moral purity, and being forthright in doctrinal matters.

2. **Checks and Balances**: Implement a system that regularly reviews the doctrinal, financial, and moral aspects of the ministry.

3. **Member Participation**: A well-informed congregation is a safeguard against the abuse of power. Frequent open forums and the practice of church discipline can be effective means of holding leaders accountable.

4. **Peer and Mentor Accountability**: Spiritual leaders should be willing to subject themselves to the scrutiny and counsel of peers and mentors in the faith.

Potential Challenges and Remedies

1. **Resistance to Accountability**: There may be resistance both from within the leadership and the congregation to enforce accountability. The remedy is ongoing education and a consistent appeal to the Scriptures to underscore its importance.
2. **False Accusations**: Leaders may be the target of false accusations. A robust and transparent accountability process will often serve to exonerate the innocent.
3. **Cover-ups**: There is often the temptation to protect the institution rather than confront sin and misconduct. This undermines trust and must be avoided at all costs. "He who conceals his transgressions will not prosper, but he who confesses and forsakes them will find compassion" (Proverbs 28:13, ESV).

The accountability of spiritual leaders is not an issue to be glossed over or addressed superficially. It is deeply rooted in the nature of God, the sanctity of the Church, and the potential for human fallibility. It requires a proactive, well-defined approach that not only acknowledges the weightiness of the role of spiritual leaders but also institutes practical measures to safeguard against abuse.

Leadership within the Body of Christ is a sacred trust, and as such, demands a high level of accountability. It reflects God's own faithfulness and righteousness and serves as a testimony to the world of the divine governance of God's kingdom. Accountability is not simply about preventing error or misconduct but about promoting a culture of integrity, godliness, and above all, a fear of the Lord, which is the beginning of wisdom (Proverbs 9:10). Therefore, it should be vigorously upheld for the health and sanctification of the church and for the glory of God.

EPHESIANS 1:13 Having Heard the Word of Truth, the Gospel of Your Salvation

The Reception of Divine Truth

In Ephesians 1:13, the Apostle Paul outlines a sequence that encapsulates the Christian experience: "In him you also, when you heard the word of truth, the gospel of your salvation, and believed in him, were sealed with the promised Holy Spirit" (ESV). The verse offers a theological and practical framework for understanding how divine truth is received and what it means for the believer. This essay aims to delve into the various components of this profound verse, considering its theological underpinnings and the implications for the Christian life.

Theological Components

1. **The Word of Truth**: The phrase "word of truth" is not a nebulous concept but refers specifically to the Gospel message. This is the divine truth, standing in stark contrast to the falsehoods that pervade the world (John 14:6).

2. **The Gospel of Your Salvation**: The Gospel is termed as "the Gospel of your salvation," emphasizing its indispensable role in the redemption of humanity. The Gospel is not merely information but the power of God for salvation (Romans 1:16).

3. **Believed in Him**: The act of believing signifies more than mental assent; it involves entrusting oneself to Christ. This belief is not a human endeavor but is enabled by God's grace (Ephesians 2:8-9).

4. **Sealed with the Promised Holy Spirit**: The Holy Spirit is the seal that God places on the believer, marking them as His own and serving as a guarantee of their inheritance (2 Corinthians 1:22).

Sequence of Reception

1. **Hearing**: The initial step in the reception of divine truth is hearing it. Romans 10:17 tells us, "So faith comes from hearing, and hearing through the word of Christ" (ESV). The act of hearing implies a transmitter of the message, reinforcing the importance of evangelism and preaching.

2. **Understanding**: Hearing must lead to understanding. Many hear the Word but fail to understand it, and thus the seed falls on rocky ground (Matthew 13:19).

3. **Believing**: Understanding transitions into believing, a faith that appropriates the promises and character of God as revealed in the Gospel message.

4. **Sealing**: The final step is the sealing by the Holy Spirit, affirming the genuineness of the faith and serving as a pledge for future glory.

The Implications of Reception

1. **Assurance**: The believer can be assured of their salvation because they are sealed by the Holy Spirit. This assurance does not breed complacency but motivates the believer to "work out your own salvation with fear and trembling" (Philippians 2:12, ESV).

2. **Responsibility**: Having received the truth, there is a responsibility to abide in it (John 8:31). The truth ought to be manifest in the way the believer lives, thinks, and interacts with others.

3. **Witness**: The reception of divine truth equips the believer to be a witness. As recipients of the Gospel of salvation, Christians are commissioned to propagate this message to others (Matthew 28:19-20).

4. **Community**: Reception of divine truth is not just an individualistic event; it has communal implications. The body of Christ is built up in unity and maturity as each member receives and operates in the truth (Ephesians 4:15-16).

Challenges and Cautions

1. **Counterfeits**: In a world filled with deceptive philosophies and false gospels, discernment is necessary to distinguish the "word of truth" from error (1 John 4:1).

2. **Intellectualism**: While the Gospel is a message that engages the mind, it is not for the intellectually elite but for all. The Gospel is straightforward, needing child-like faith for its reception (Matthew 18:3).

3. **Emotionalism**: Reception of the truth is not merely an emotional experience. While emotions are involved, they are not the basis of our assurance; the Word of God is.

The reception of divine truth, as encapsulated in Ephesians 1:13, is a multifaceted experience involving hearing, understanding, believing, and being sealed by the Holy Spirit. This reception carries significant implications for assurance, responsibility, witness, and community involvement for the believer. Understanding these elements is crucial for personal sanctification and effective Christian service. Therefore, let us heed the instruction of Proverbs 23:23: "Buy truth, and do not sell it; buy wisdom, instruction, and understanding" (ESV). The reception of divine truth is not a mere event but an ongoing process, a continual investment in a life committed to glorifying God and enjoying Him forever.

The Gospel as the Word of Truth

As Paul writes in Ephesians 1:13, "In him you also, when you heard the word of truth, the gospel of your salvation, and believed in him, were sealed with the promised Holy Spirit" (ESV). The concept that the Gospel is "the word of truth" bears immense significance both theologically and practically. This essay will focus on unpacking the notion of the Gospel as the word of truth, with attention to its foundational doctrines, its unique characteristics, and its transformative power in the lives of believers.

The Gospel Defined

The term "Gospel" originates from the Greek word "euangelion," meaning "good news." In a Christian context, it refers to the message concerning Jesus Christ's life, death, and resurrection for the purpose of providing salvation to all who believe (1 Corinthians 15:1-4).

The Gospel and Truth

1. **Inerrancy**: The Gospel is true because it is rooted in the inerrant Word of God (2 Timothy 3:16-17). Therefore, every statement and doctrine it contains can be trusted completely.

2. **Exclusivity**: Jesus states, "I am the way, and the truth, and the life. No one comes to the Father except through me" (John 14:6, ESV). The Gospel is the exclusive avenue through which truth about God and salvation can be known.

3. **Objectivity**: The Gospel is not subject to human opinions or cultural norms. It stands as an objective reality revealed by God Himself (Galatians 1:11-12).

Foundational Doctrines of the Gospel

1. **Deity of Christ**: One of the core doctrines is the deity of Christ. Jesus is not just a moral teacher but God incarnate (John 1:1, 14).

2. **Sinfulness of Humanity**: The Gospel hinges on the premise that all have sinned and are in need of salvation (Romans 3:23).

3. **Substitutionary Atonement**: Jesus died on the cross as a substitute for sinners, taking the penalty that we deserve (Isaiah 53:4-6).

4. **Resurrection**: Christ's resurrection is the guarantee of our own future resurrection and the cornerstone of the Christian faith (1 Corinthians 15:17).

Characteristics of the Gospel as the Word of Truth

1. **Clarity**: The Gospel is straightforward enough for a child to understand. This doesn't negate the depth and the complexities that can be explored, but its basic truths are simple (Matthew 18:3).
2. **Unchangeable**: Truth, by its nature, is unalterable. Similarly, the Gospel remains the same yesterday, today, and forever (Hebrews 13:8).
3. **Universal Application**: The Gospel is for all people, regardless of culture, age, or background (Revelation 7:9).
4. **Actionable**: The Gospel is not merely to be intellectually assented to but lived out, demonstrating its truth through a transformed life (James 2:14-17).

The Transformative Power of the Gospel

1. **Regeneration**: The Gospel is not just a proclamation; it's the power of God for the transformation of the believer (Titus 3:5).
2. **Sanctification**: The truth of the Gospel sanctifies believers, aligning them more closely with God's character and will (John 17:17).
3. **Service**: The Gospel compels the believer into action, to serve both God and neighbor in love (Galatians 5:13).
4. **Hope**: The Gospel provides hope, not just for this life but for eternity (1 Peter 1:3-4).

Challenges and Caveats

1. **The Gospel and Culture**: In a relativistic society, the exclusivity of the Gospel can be perceived as offensive or intolerant. Christians must be prepared to defend the objectivity of the Gospel (1 Peter 3:15).
2. **Legalism and Licentiousness**: There's a danger of drifting into legalism, where the Gospel is equated with rule-keeping, or licentiousness, where grace is abused (Romans 6:1-2; Galatians 5:1).
3. **Compromise**: There's a temptation to water down the Gospel to make it more palatable. Such compromise is a betrayal of the truth (Galatians 1:6-9).

The Gospel is not just any word; it is the "word of truth," the only message that can genuinely lead to salvation. Its inerrancy, exclusivity, and objectivity set it apart from all human philosophies and religions. Its foundational doctrines provide the framework for understanding God, the world, and ourselves. Its unique characteristics ensure its relevance and applicability to every culture and generation.

Ultimately, the Gospel is not just to be believed but to be lived. Its transformative power changes us from the inside out, equipping us for service and filling us with an eternal hope that the world cannot offer. Therefore, let us stand firm in this word of truth, boldly proclaiming it and faithfully living it out, for the glory of God and the salvation of souls.

The Personal Nature of Salvation

The concept of salvation in Christian theology is often framed in collective terms—a community of believers, the Church, being saved. While the corporate aspect is biblical and essential, the Scriptures also emphasize that salvation is a deeply personal experience between the individual and God. The phrase "work out your own salvation with fear and trembling" from Philippians 2:12 (ESV) aptly captures this personal dimension. This essay will delve into the personal nature of salvation, looking at its foundational principles, essential elements, and implications for the individual believer.

Foundational Principles of Personal Salvation

1. **God's Initiative**: Salvation begins with God, who took the first step towards reconciling humanity to Himself through Christ (John 3:16). His love and grace are not merely abstract concepts but are personally directed at each individual (Galatians 2:20).

2. **Human Responsibility**: While salvation is a gift from God, it requires a personal response from the individual. Free will plays a crucial role in accepting or rejecting God's gift (Joshua 24:15).

3. **Individual Accountability**: Each person will stand before God and give an account of their life (Romans 14:12). Salvation is not inherited or automatically conferred through family or community.

Essential Elements of Personal Salvation

1. **Faith**: The individual must personally place faith in Jesus Christ for salvation. Faith is not merely intellectual assent but involves trusting Christ for forgiveness of sins and eternal life (Ephesians 2:8-9).

2. **Repentance**: Genuine repentance involves a personal acknowledgment of sin, a turning away from it, and a turning towards God (Luke 13:3).

3. **Confession**: The mouth confesses what the heart believes. Personal confession of Jesus as Lord is a crucial aspect of salvation (Romans 10:9-10).

4. **Regeneration**: The individual experiences a new birth, not of flesh and blood but of the Spirit. This regeneration results in a new nature and a new life in Christ (John 3:3).

5. **Sanctification**: This is the lifelong process where the believer is increasingly conformed to the likeness of Christ (1 Thessalonians 4:3). Sanctification is both a corporate experience within the Body of Christ and an intensely personal journey.

Implications for the Individual Believer

1. **Personal Relationship**: Salvation facilitates a personal relationship with God. The believer is not just a servant but a child of God (Romans 8:15-17).

2. **Identity in Christ**: Understanding one's personal salvation solidifies their identity in Christ, separate from the roles, stereotypes, and expectations that the world may impose (Galatians 2:20).

3. **Purpose and Calling**: With personal salvation comes a personal calling. Each believer is equipped with unique gifts for service and is accountable for using them for God's glory (1 Corinthians 12:7).

4. **Holiness**: Personal salvation leads to personal holiness. Each believer is called to live out a holy life as a testimony to God's transforming power (1 Peter 1:15-16).

5. **Eternal Security**: Salvation is not merely a ticket to heaven but a transformational experience that affects the individual for eternity (John 10:28-29). However, salvation requires ongoing faith and obedience, with no assurance of "once saved, always saved" (Hebrews 6:4-6).

Challenges and Caveats

1. **Self-Centeredness**: The personal aspect of salvation should not lead to self-centered Christianity, neglecting the corporate identity and mission of the Church.

2. **Legalism and Licentiousness**: The freedom that comes with understanding one's personal salvation should not devolve into legalism or licentiousness (Galatians 5:13).

3. **False Assurance**: A merely intellectual acknowledgment without a transformed life may give false assurance of salvation (James 2:19).

The personal nature of salvation is a profound and multifaceted doctrine that carries significant implications for the individual believer. From its foundational principles of God's initiative and human responsibility to its essential elements like faith, repentance, and sanctification, personal salvation is not a one-size-fits-all experience but a tailored journey with God. The implications of this are transformative, providing a personal relationship with God, a robust sense of identity, a unique calling, and a life of holiness. These blessings come with responsibilities—to live a Christ-honoring life, to use one's gifts for the glory of God, and to persist in faith and obedience. Therefore, understanding the personal nature of salvation is crucial for every believer, serving as both an encouragement and a challenge to live a life fully devoted to God.

The Assurance of Faith

The doctrine of the assurance of faith has been a matter of great concern for countless Christians throughout history. The question often asked is, "How can I know for sure that I am saved?" The Scriptures offer a robust answer to this question, affirming that assurance is not only possible but should be the experience of every true believer. This essay aims to delve into the biblical underpinnings of this assurance, the indicators of genuine faith, and the implications for the Christian life.

Biblical Foundation for Assurance

1. **Direct Promise from God**: The Bible clearly states that whoever believes in Jesus Christ has eternal life (John 3:16). When we take God at His word, we have a basis for assurance. 1 John 5:11-13 tells us that we can know we have eternal life if we have believed in the Son of God.

2. **Witness of the Spirit**: Romans 8:16 declares that "The Spirit Himself bears witness with our spirit that we are children of God." While the Holy Spirit may not indwell us, His role as the agent behind the inspired Scriptures assures us when we reflect on the Word of God.

3. **Unchanging Nature of God**: Hebrews 6:17-18 tells us that it is impossible for God to lie. Therefore, His promises are immutable, providing a solid ground for assurance.

Indicators of Genuine Faith

1. **Continued Belief in Christ**: True assurance comes when there is a continued faith in Jesus Christ as Lord and Savior. A fleeting moment of belief is not the basis for assurance; rather, ongoing faith is (Colossians 1:23).

2. **Obedience to God's Word**: Jesus said, "If you love me, you will keep my commandments" (John 14:15, ESV). A life characterized by obedience to God is a sign of genuine faith.

3. **Love for the Brethren**: 1 John 3:14 affirms that love for fellow Christians is an indicator of having passed from death to life.

4. **Moral Uprightness**: While no Christian is sinless, a life marked by moral and ethical integrity, as opposed to habitual sin, indicates genuine faith (1 John 3:6-9).

5. **Endurance in Trials**: James 1:12 blesses the one who remains steadfast under trial. Such endurance is not only a sign of genuine faith but also serves to strengthen assurance.

Implications for the Christian Life

1. **Confidence in Witnessing**: Assurance brings a sense of confidence in sharing the Gospel. A Christian who is sure of his or her salvation will be more eager to tell others about Christ.

2. **Strength in Adversity**: Knowing that one is securely in the hands of God brings strength during times of adversity. Paul's words in Romans 8:38-39 make it clear that nothing can separate us from the love of God in Christ Jesus.

3. **Motivation for Holiness**: Assurance should not lead to complacency but rather to a greater desire to live a holy life. Titus 2:11-14 explains that the grace of God trains us to renounce ungodliness.

4. **Comfort in Doubt**: Even the most steadfast believers can go through periods of doubt. The principles of assurance serve as an anchor during such times, reminding us to focus on the objective truth of God's Word over subjective feelings.

Pitfalls and Warnings

1. **False Assurance**: There's a danger in thinking one is saved when they are not. Matthew 7:21-23 provides a sobering warning about those who think they are saved but lack a true relationship with Christ.

2. **Misuse of Assurance**: Assurance should not be taken as a license for sin. The doctrine of "once saved, always saved" or eternal security is not biblically supported. We are warned in Hebrews 3:12 about the deceitfulness of sin and the possibility of falling away from the living God.

3. **Overemphasis on Feelings**: Assurance based solely on emotional experiences can be unstable. Faith must be rooted in the objective truths of Scripture.

The assurance of faith is a rich biblical doctrine that provides immense comfort, motivation, and strength to the believer. This assurance is rooted in the promises of God, witnessed by the Spirit through the Word, and evidenced by the fruits of genuine faith. While there are pitfalls to be wary of, such as false assurance and the misuse of this doctrine, understanding the biblical basis and implications of assurance can bring a profound sense of joy and peace to the Christian's life. Hence, every believer should seek to understand, experience, and live in the light of this assurance, making their calling and election sure (2 Peter 1:10), and thus enriching their walk with God.

2 TIMOTHY 2:15 Rightly Handling the Word of Truth

The Responsibility of Scripture Handling

The Apostle Paul's solemn charge to Timothy in 2 Timothy 2:15, "Do your best to present yourself to God as one approved, a worker who has no need to be ashamed, rightly handling the word of truth" (ESV), stands as a clarion call to all who seek to be faithful stewards of the divine revelation. The text delineates the immense responsibility and skill required in handling the Scriptures, marking it as a non-negotiable aspect of Christian service and discipleship. This essay seeks to explore the various facets of this biblical directive, underscoring its timeless importance and practical ramifications.

Biblical Context of the Passage

1. **Historical Setting**: Paul writes from a Roman prison, fully aware that his end is near (2 Timothy 4:6). He pens these words as a final exhortation to Timothy, his spiritual son and pastor of the church in Ephesus.

2. **Immediate Context**: The preceding verses in 2 Timothy 2 discuss various analogies to describe a faithful Christian worker—one who is like a soldier, an athlete, and a farmer. Paul builds on these illustrations to emphasize the critical role of accurately interpreting and applying the Scriptures.

The Charge Explained

1. **"Do your best to present yourself to God"**: This calls for diligence and earnestness. The task is not merely academic; it's spiritual, requiring deep devotion to God.

2. **"As one approved"**: The Greek word translated "approved" (*dokimos*) means tested and proven, underlining the vetting process that comes through meticulous engagement with the Scriptures.

3. **"A worker who has no need to be ashamed"**: A person who mishandles the Scriptures will eventually bring disgrace not only to themselves but also, indirectly, to the God they claim to serve.

4. **"Rightly handling the word of truth"**: The Greek word for "rightly handling" (*orthotomounta*) implies cutting straight, as a workman precisely cuts

a piece of material. The notion here is one of presenting Scripture correctly and clearly.

The Imperatives of Rightly Handling Scripture

1. **Hermeneutical Integrity**: Approaching the text with an objective historical-grammatical method of interpretation ensures that we draw out its original meaning rather than reading our preferences into it.

2. **Doctrinal Purity**: A proper interpretation of Scripture will lead to sound doctrine, as espoused in texts like Titus 2:1. In an age of doctrinal laxity, this is paramount.

3. **Personal Holiness**: James 1:22-25 stresses the need for being doers of the Word, not just hearers. Correctly handling Scripture must translate into a life of integrity and godliness.

4. **Teaching with Precision**: Those in positions of teaching have the added responsibility to transmit the Scriptures accurately to their listeners (James 3:1). This involves thorough preparation and a deep reverence for the text.

5. **Apologetic Readiness**: The ability to defend one's faith (1 Peter 3:15) is considerably enhanced when one has a strong grasp of the Scriptures.

Pitfalls in Scripture Handling

1. **Subjectivism**: A failure to hold to an objective standard of interpretation can lead to subjective, often incorrect, conclusions.

2. **Cherry-Picking**: Selectively quoting passages out of context to support a preconceived belief undermines the integrity of the Scripture.

3. **Theological Biases**: Imposing external theological systems on the text can lead to distorted interpretations. The Bible should be allowed to speak for itself.

4. **Negligence**: A lackadaisical attitude towards study and preparation will invariably result in poor handling of the Word.

Consequences of Mishandling Scripture

1. **Spiritual Deception**: Incorrectly interpreting Scripture can lead oneself and others into doctrinal error and ultimately away from the faith.

2. **Dishonor to God**: Jehovah is dishonored when His Word is twisted or misrepresented.

3. **Loss of Witness**: Credibility in the eyes of the world and effectiveness in evangelism are compromised when Scripture is mishandled.

The charge to rightly handle the Word of truth is not just a pastoral duty but a Christian obligation. It comes with the need for intellectual rigor, spiritual discipline, and a humble dependence on God for wisdom and insight. The stakes are high—both the honor of God and the well-being of His people hang in the balance. Therefore, it is a task that must be undertaken with the utmost seriousness and dedication. In fulfilling this mandate, the Christian worker finds themselves approved by God, unashamed in their labor, and enriched in their walk with Christ.

The Importance of Accurate Interpretation

"Do your best to present yourself to God as one approved, a worker who has no need to be ashamed, rightly handling the word of truth" (2 Timothy 2:15, ESV). This verse serves as a poignant reminder of the significant responsibility resting upon each individual who engages with the Scriptures. Accurate interpretation is not a mere scholarly endeavor but a sacred obligation. It serves as a foundational pillar upon which rests the integrity of Christian doctrine, practice, and witness. This essay aims to elucidate the manifold reasons why accurate interpretation is indispensable to a robust Christian life and theology.

The Divine Origin of Scripture

The starting point of our discussion must be the divine origin of Scripture. 2 Timothy 3:16 asserts that "All Scripture is breathed out by God and profitable for teaching, for reproof, for correction, and for training in righteousness." This divine inspiration sets the Bible apart from any other piece of literature; it is God's revelation to humanity. Therefore, when we engage with the Bible, we are, in essence, engaging with God Himself. This engagement requires a level of respect, diligence, and humility that is fitting to its Author.

Consequences of Inaccurate Interpretation

Misinterpretation of Scripture can have far-reaching implications, not only for the individual interpreter but also for the broader Christian community.

1. **Doctrinal Error**: The gravest consequence is doctrinal deviation. A misreading of Scripture can lead to heretical beliefs that can be spiritually damaging. Errant teachings on subjects such as the nature of God, the deity of Christ, and the means of salvation can have eternal repercussions.

2. **Moral Slippage**: Misunderstanding God's commands or principles can lead to unethical decisions and actions, tarnishing the testimony of the Church and leading people away from the faith.

3. **Disunity in the Body of Christ**: Erroneous interpretations can foster division and discord among believers, leading to the fragmentation of the Church.

The Role of Hermeneutics

Hermeneutics, or the science of interpretation, provides a set of guidelines and principles for extracting the original meaning of the text. Given that we are dedicated to an objective historical-grammatical method, our aim is to discern what the biblical authors intended to convey to their original audience.

1. **Historical Context**: Understanding the historical background, including the culture, politics, and societal norms of the time, aids in grasping the intent of the Scripture.
2. **Grammatical Analysis**: A thorough examination of the language, including syntax, word choices, and sentence structure, illuminates the precise meaning of the text.
3. **Literary Genres**: Recognizing the type of literature—whether historical narrative, poetry, epistle, or apocalyptic—helps in applying appropriate interpretive methods.
4. **Theology**: While we steer clear of reading any external theological system into the text, the immediate and broader biblical context must inform our interpretation.

Interpretive Challenges

1. **Cultural Gap**: The biblical world is culturally distant from our modern setting, which can sometimes lead to misunderstandings if not carefully bridged.
2. **Language Barrier**: The Scriptures were written in Hebrew, Aramaic, and Greek. Working from translations requires extra caution to ensure fidelity to the original languages.
3. **Preconceived Notions**: All readers come to the text with a set of presuppositions. These must be consciously set aside to allow the text to speak for itself.

Practical Outcomes of Accurate Interpretation

1. **Personal Edification**: Rightly interpreting the Word leads to spiritual growth, a deeper understanding of God's character, and transformation into the likeness of Christ.

2. **Effective Ministry**: Ministers equipped with accurate biblical understanding are more effective in teaching, counseling, and leading the Church.

3. **Apologetic Impact**: In a world skeptical of Christianity, accurate interpretation prepares believers to give a reasoned defense for the hope that is within them (1 Peter 3:15).

4. **Evangelistic Authenticity**: A correct understanding of the Gospel message is pivotal for authentic evangelistic outreach.

The task of accurate interpretation is not a luxury or an option; it is an imperative. The Scriptures, as the Word of God, demand nothing less than our most rigorous intellectual and spiritual efforts to understand them correctly. In doing so, we honor God, build up the Church, and become effective witnesses in a world that is increasingly hostile to the message of the Bible. Therefore, as we seek to "rightly handle the word of truth," let us do so with the reverence and earnestness befitting the high calling we have received.

Skills for Truthful Exegesis

The call to "rightly divide the word of truth" (2 Timothy 2:15, ESV) serves as an admonition for every Christian, especially for those entrusted with the solemn task of teaching and preaching. Exegesis, the critical explanation or interpretation of a text, specifically the Scriptures, is central to fulfilling this responsibility. Truthful exegesis not only respects the inspired text but ensures the effective communication of divine truths to the Church and the world. This article will explore the necessary skills for executing a faithful, truthful exegesis of the Bible.

The Contextual Approach

Understanding the context is the foundation of any exegesis. The aim is to situate the passage within its broader narrative or argumentative structure.

1. **Immediate Context**: This is the setting immediately surrounding a passage. What precedes and follows the passage helps illuminate its purpose and meaning.

2. **Overall Context**: This is the broader scope within which a book of the Bible was written. It includes understanding the themes, arguments, and flow of thought throughout the book.

Linguistic Competency

1. **Language Proficiency**: While not everyone can be a scholar in Hebrew, Aramaic, and Greek, some basic familiarity can be enormously helpful.

2. **Word Studies**: Words are the building blocks of meaning. A careful study of the key terms, their nuances, and their uses elsewhere in Scripture can be illuminating.

3. **Syntax and Sentence Structure**: These often carry important theological weight. For example, the use of the subjunctive in conditional sentences may express the uncertainty of a situation, which can be essential for understanding a passage's intent.

Historical Background

1. **Cultural Understanding**: Customs, norms, and social structures often underlie the biblical text. Knowing these can prevent anachronistic interpretations.

2. **Geographical Knowledge**: Places and locations sometimes carry symbolic value or practical implications for understanding a text.

3. **Time Period**: Different eras in biblical history had different challenges, norms, and practices. Knowing the historical time frame aids in understanding the issues being addressed.

Literary Analysis

1. **Genre Identification**: The Bible contains various genres, each with its specific conventions that must be considered in interpretation.

2. **Textual Structure**: Understanding the organization of the text—be it a chiasm, parallelism, or other forms—can reveal the emphasis and key points of a passage.

Theological Coherence

1. **Canonical Consistency**: Scripture does not contradict Scripture. Interpreting a passage in the context of the entire canon ensures doctrinal consistency.

2. **Major Themes**: Identifying major theological themes in a passage, especially as they relate to core doctrines, is vital for faithful interpretation.

Logical Reasoning

1. **Arguments and Flow of Thought**: Following the logical progression in a passage helps understand its intended message.

2. **Implications**: Understanding what a text implies, along with what it explicitly states, is essential for capturing its full message.

Practical Relevance

1. **Application**: Accurate exegesis must be geared toward applying the text in today's context without violating its original intent.
2. **Ethical and Moral Relevance**: The Bible often addresses ethical and moral issues. Accurate exegesis helps ensure that biblical ethics are faithfully represented and applied.

Humility and Prayer

The process of exegesis is not just an intellectual exercise but a spiritual discipline. The interpreter must approach the text with humility, recognizing the possibility of human error and biases. Prayer is crucial for inviting the guidance of the Holy Spirit, who inspired the text.

Consultation of Trusted Resources

While it's important to let the text speak for itself, consultation of trusted commentaries and scholarly works can provide valuable insights and help in avoiding interpretive pitfalls. Given that we're adhering to a conservative approach, one should consult resources that are aligned with a high view of Scripture and orthodox Christian doctrine.

Exegesis is a rigorous yet rewarding endeavor, demanding a diverse skill set ranging from linguistic abilities to theological acumen. Yet at its core, the aim is simple yet profound: to understand and convey God's truth as revealed in His Word. Each skill we hone in service to this goal serves not just our intellectual curiosity but our spiritual formation, equipping us to fulfill our call to be diligent workmen, unashamed and well-equipped to handle the truth of God's Word.

Accountability Before God in Teaching

The role of a teacher, particularly one who instructs in the matters of faith and Scripture, carries with it a significant level of responsibility and accountability. The Bible is unambiguous in its insistence that those who teach are held to a high standard before God. James 3:1 sternly warns, "Not many of you should become teachers, my brothers, for you know that we who teach will be judged with greater strictness" (ESV). This article aims to expound upon the weight of this accountability and to highlight the crucial aspects that teachers must bear in mind as they undertake this sacred task.

The Weight of Words

One of the most immediate aspects of teaching is the use of words, whether spoken or written. Words have the power to build up, and they also have the power to destroy. Teachers must weigh their words carefully, recognizing that they can either lead people toward truth or astray into error. Proverbs 18:21 reminds us, "Death and life are in the power of the tongue" (ESV). Teachers must be conscientious, ensuring that what they articulate aligns with the whole counsel of God as revealed in Scripture.

The Integrity of Doctrine

Second Timothy 4:3-4 paints a vivid picture of a time when people will not endure sound teaching but will seek out teachers to suit their own desires. This prophetic warning should be a sobering reminder that fidelity to correct doctrine is not an optional luxury but an obligatory necessity for teachers. They must avoid the temptation to adjust or dilute biblical teachings to make them more palatable to their audience. The integrity of doctrine should be sacrosanct, never compromised for the sake of popularity or convenience.

Hermeneutical Responsibility

Linked closely with doctrinal integrity is the responsibility to rightly handle the Word of God (2 Timothy 2:15). Teachers are accountable for interpreting Scripture accurately and faithfully, adhering to sound hermeneutical principles. This entails a deep commitment to understanding the original languages, historical contexts, and literary genres found in the Bible. Anything less jeopardizes the truth and risks misleading those who listen. Therefore, rigorous training and ongoing study are not merely beneficial; they are imperative for anyone who assumes the role of a teacher.

Spiritual Maturity and Moral Uprightness

The Apostle Paul, in his pastoral epistles, emphasizes the necessity of spiritual maturity and moral uprightness in leaders. For instance, the qualifications listed in 1 Timothy 3:1-7 and Titus 1:5-9 underscore the importance of a blameless life, marked by self-control, humility, and integrity. Teachers are to exemplify the very principles and virtues they expound from the Scriptures. Their lives should be an open book of what it means to walk in obedience and faithfulness to God's Word.

The Stewardship of Influence

Teachers inherently possess influence over their audience. This is a form of stewardship that God entrusts to them, and they will be accountable for how they wield this influence. The Apostle Paul spoke of the stewardship of the mysteries of God and insisted that stewards must be found trustworthy (1 Corinthians 4:1-2). Teachers should constantly evaluate whether their influence is drawing people closer to Christ and deeper into truth or leading them down paths of confusion and error.

The Importance of Humility

Humility is essential for teachers because it serves as a safeguard against the potential pitfalls of pride and arrogance. Recognizing that they are not infallible interpreters of God's Word, teachers should maintain a posture of humility, willing to be corrected and to adjust their understanding as they grow in their knowledge of the Scriptures. Moreover, humility enables teachers to acknowledge that they are merely instruments in the hands of God, entirely dependent on His grace for their ministry's effectiveness.

Prayer and Dependence on God

Given the weight of their task, teachers must be individuals committed to prayer and dependent on God. They should earnestly seek the wisdom that comes from above, asking for the Holy Spirit's guidance as they study and convey the Scriptures. As Paul stated, "our sufficiency is from God, who has made us sufficient to be ministers of a new covenant" (2 Corinthians 3:5-6, ESV).

The role of a teacher in the body of Christ is a lofty and noble task, yet it comes with grave responsibilities. The need for doctrinal integrity, sound hermeneutics, spiritual and moral uprightness, wise stewardship, humility, and prayerful dependence on God are non-negotiable aspects of this ministry. Teachers must always bear in mind that they will stand accountable before God for the souls they are guiding. This realization should drive them to discharge their duties with the utmost faithfulness, reverence, and godly fear, to the glory of God and the edification of His people.

HEBREWS 10:26 If We Go on Sinning Deliberately after Receiving the Accurate Knowledge of the Truth

The Gravity of Deliberate Sin

The Letter to the Hebrews is a rich theological treatise that presents the high-priestly ministry of Jesus Christ as the superior and ultimate fulfillment of the Old Testament sacrificial system. Its primary audience consists of Jewish believers who are tempted to revert to the rituals of Judaism. The author of Hebrews exhorts them to persevere in faith, issuing strong warnings against apostasy. Among these is the solemn caution in Hebrews 10:26: "For if we go on sinning deliberately after receiving the knowledge of the truth, there no longer remains a sacrifice for sins" (ESV).

The Context of the Warning

Understanding the weight of this verse requires apprehending its immediate and broader context. The preceding verses (Hebrews 10:19-25) underscore the new and living way to God made possible by the blood of Jesus. The author encourages believers to hold fast to their confession and to stir up one another to love and good works. The section that follows our verse discusses the severe consequences for those who reject the message and commit willful sin. Thus, the placement of this warning serves as a pivotal point, urging the audience to be vigilant in their faith walk.

Defining "Knowledge of the Truth"

The phrase "knowledge of the truth" in the verse carries specific connotations. In biblical parlance, "truth" refers to the divine revelation contained in Scripture, and "knowledge" implies not mere intellectual assent but a deep, experiential understanding. It is the accurate knowledge of God's will and purpose as revealed through Jesus Christ and the apostolic teaching. This is a knowledge that brings moral and spiritual responsibility. Ignorance may be excusable, but deliberate sin after gaining such insight is indefensible.

The Nature of "Deliberate" Sin

It is crucial to distinguish between inadvertent sin and deliberate sin. All believers struggle with sin, often falling short despite sincere efforts to obey God. However, the sin in view here is not accidental but premeditated and persistent. It is sin committed with a high hand, even after one has understood the divine injunctions against it. This represents a hardened state of rebellion and manifests a heart that has turned away from God.

The Implication of "No Longer Remains a Sacrifice"

The phrase "there no longer remains a sacrifice for sins" should be interpreted in the context of the entire argument of Hebrews. The book argues for the finality and sufficiency of Christ's sacrifice, which has forever replaced the repetitive sacrifices of the Old Covenant. If one rejects this ultimate sacrifice through persistent and deliberate sin, there is nothing else that can atone for such disobedience.

The Terrible Consequences

The author spells out the consequences in verses 27-31, drawing from Old Testament imagery of divine judgment. Rejecting the knowledge of the truth and embracing willful sin invites nothing less than "a fearful expectation of judgment, and a fury of fire" (Hebrews 10:27, ESV). The passage underscores the gravity of the offense by comparing it to the punishment meted out under the Mosaic Law, emphasizing that defiance against the New Covenant warrants even more severe retribution.

The Role of Conscience and Repentance

It's important to note that the passage does not deny the possibility of repentance. However, it suggests that a continuous lifestyle of deliberate sin dulls the conscience and hardens the heart, making repentance increasingly unlikely. The believer is urged to heed the promptings of a God-informed conscience, which, if ignored repeatedly, may cease to warn against impending spiritual danger.

A Call to Persevere

The sobering warning is ultimately aimed at urging believers to persevere in the faith. The broader context of Hebrews includes not just warnings but also exhortations and encouragements to press on to maturity (Hebrews 6:1), to draw near to the throne of grace with confidence (Hebrews 4:16), and to consider Jesus, the founder and perfecter of our faith (Hebrews 12:2).

Hebrews 10:26 serves as a grave caution against taking lightly the obligations and responsibilities that come with the knowledge of divine truth. The Christian journey is not a casual undertaking but a committed relationship with God, sealed by the blood of Christ, which requires steadfastness and obedience. Deliberate sin is an affront to the grace of God and invites severe consequences, including the fearful expectation of judgment. Therefore, let this warning prompt us to examine our lives, to repent of any willful disobedience, and to cling more tightly to our great High Priest, Jesus Christ, who alone can help us in our time of need.

The Role of Accurate Knowledge

In the life of a Christian, few things hold as much weight as possessing accurate knowledge of God's Word. Scripture calls upon us to not be "children, tossed to and fro by the waves and carried about by every wind of doctrine" (Ephesians 4:14, ESV). In a world awash with misinformation and shifting moral landscapes, the significance of obtaining and applying accurate knowledge cannot be overstated. It is the linchpin that holds together our understanding of God, our spiritual walk, and our eternal destiny.

Accurate Knowledge Distinguished from General Awareness

It is essential to distinguish between mere awareness or superficial familiarity and accurate knowledge. In the biblical context, the term 'knowledge' often encompasses more than just intellectual data. It involves deep understanding, appreciation, and the resultant transformation. It's not mere possession but application that counts, as James 1:22 advises us not to be "hearers only, deceiving yourselves" but to be doers of the Word. Accurate knowledge is not optional; it's the gateway to discernment and wisdom.

The Role in Spiritual Maturity

The Apostle Paul frequently underscores the importance of mature understanding in matters of faith. In Colossians 1:9-10, Paul prays that the believers might be "filled with the knowledge of [God's] will in all spiritual wisdom and understanding," so as to walk in a manner worthy of the Lord. Accurate knowledge, in this context, is a precursor to spiritual wisdom and ethical living. It allows us to discern what is "the good and acceptable and perfect will of God" (Romans 12:2, ESV).

The Importance for Salvation

Accurate knowledge is not only vital for spiritual growth but also for the most fundamental of all Christian experiences: salvation. In 2 Timothy 3:15, Paul reminds Timothy that "the sacred writings...are able to make you wise for salvation through faith in Christ Jesus." The Word of God is not merely a collection of stories and moral teachings; it is the revelation that leads us to salvation when understood correctly.

The Shield Against False Teachings

One of the immediate benefits of accurate knowledge is its role as a safeguard against heresies and false doctrines. Apostolic warnings against false teachers are a recurrent theme in the New Testament. The Apostle John advises testing the spirits to see whether they are from God (1 John 4:1), and Paul exhorts Timothy to rightly handle the "word of truth" (2 Timothy 2:15, ESV). Accurate knowledge equips us to discern truth from error, preventing us from being "tossed to and fro" by every new teaching that comes our way.

Accurate Knowledge and Ethical Conduct

The relationship between accurate knowledge and ethical conduct is inextricable. In 1 Timothy 1:5, Paul states that "The aim of our charge is love that issues from a pure heart and a good conscience and a sincere faith." These virtues are fruits of a life informed and guided by accurate knowledge. Ignorance might be bliss in some worldly matters, but in spiritual matters, it leads to ethical and doctrinal pitfalls.

The Source of Accurate Knowledge

For Christians, the ultimate source of accurate knowledge is Scripture, which is "breathed out by God and profitable for teaching, for reproof, for correction, and for training in righteousness" (2 Timothy 3:16, ESV). Through the teachings of the apostles and prophets, and supremely through Jesus Christ—the Word incarnate—we receive divine, trustworthy knowledge.

The Responsibility that Comes with Knowledge

It's important to note that accurate knowledge brings with it responsibility. Jesus said, "Everyone to whom much was given, of him much will be required" (Luke 12:48, ESV). With the precious resource of God's revealed truth comes the obligation to live it out, to proclaim it, and to defend it.

The Limitations of Human Understanding

While acknowledging the essential role of accurate knowledge, we must also recognize our finite ability to fully comprehend the infinite God. As Deuteronomy 29:29 states, "The secret things belong to the Lord our God, but the things that are revealed belong to us and to our children forever, that we may do all the words of this law." Our focus should be on what has been revealed and can be understood, which is sufficient for faith and practice.

Accurate knowledge is indispensable in the Christian life for various reasons: it fosters spiritual maturity, it safeguards against false doctrines, it plays an integral role in salvation, and it underpins ethical living. The quest for it should be relentless, and the application of it should be meticulous. In a world where truth is often considered relative, the Christian's commitment to accurate knowledge stands as a testimony to the unchanging nature of God's Word and His character. The Scripture remains the ultimate source of this knowledge, divinely designed to make us "complete, equipped for every good work" (2 Timothy 3:17, ESV). Therefore, let us strive to obtain, guard, and apply accurate knowledge to the glory of God.

The Intersection of Truth and Accountability

Accountability and truth are two foundational pillars in the Christian life. While truth refers to the unchanging realities revealed in God's Word, accountability points toward the personal responsibility of aligning one's life in accordance with that truth. Often, these two concepts are viewed in isolation, but Scripture presents a robust theology where truth and accountability intersect and inform one another. In this exploration, we will look at the interconnectedness of these two critical concepts and how they function together to advance the Christian's spiritual maturity and witness.

The Inherent Connection

From the outset, it's essential to understand that truth is not merely a set of propositional statements or doctrinal creeds. In the Christian context, truth is the revealed will and character of God, most perfectly demonstrated in Jesus Christ, who said, "I am the way, and the truth, and the life" (John 14:6, ESV). Thus, truth is relational at its core. And because it is relational, it naturally implies accountability—a commitment to align one's thoughts, words, and actions in accordance with this revealed truth.

Truth as the Foundation of Accountability

Accountability, in any meaningful sense, cannot exist without a recognized standard of truth. Paul reminded Timothy that Scripture is "profitable for teaching, for reproof, for correction, and for training in righteousness" (2 Timothy 3:16, ESV). Without a standard of truth, accountability becomes an aimless exercise, devoid of direction or purpose.

Accountability in the Presence of Truth

Just as truth forms the basis for accountability, so does accountability give expression to truth. Knowing the truth calls for an actionable response. James warns against being "hearers only, deceiving yourselves" (James 1:22, ESV). We are to live out the truths we claim to believe; otherwise, we may find ourselves in the dangerous position of professing faith without possessing it (Matthew 7:21-23).

The Role of the Christian Community

Accountability is often fostered within the community of believers. Paul instructs the Galatians to "bear one another's burdens" (Galatians 6:2, ESV). Here, the understanding and application of truth become communal activities, as believers encourage, exhort, and sometimes rebuke each other in love (Colossians 3:16). This shared responsibility promotes a culture of accountability, where truth is not just believed but lived.

Accountability and Spiritual Growth

Where there is a commitment to truth and a system of accountability, spiritual growth occurs. Peter advises believers to "grow in the grace and knowledge of our Lord and Savior Jesus Christ" (2 Peter 3:18, ESV). The intersection of truth and accountability serves as the fertile ground for spiritual maturation. When Christians hold themselves and each other accountable to the truth of Scripture, they build a spiritually robust community that reflects Christ's teachings.

The Challenges of Truth and Accountability

While the relationship between truth and accountability is symbiotic, it is not without its challenges. The most significant obstacle may be the human propensity toward sin, which can make us resist both truth and accountability. Often, pride, fear, or rebellion can prevent us from fully embracing these principles, thereby stunting our spiritual growth.

The Question of Judgment

In a society that often misconstrues judgment as inherently negative, the biblical approach to accountability is countercultural. Scripture encourages wise judgment, primarily when rooted in a love for truth and for the individual being corrected (Matthew 7:1-5; Proverbs 27:5-6). Therefore, judgment, when correctly executed, serves to uphold truth and foster accountability among believers.

The Eternal Implications

The impact of truth and accountability extends beyond our temporal existence. The choices we make and the doctrines we adhere to have eternal consequences. Revelation speaks of a final judgment where "the dead were judged by what was written in the books, according to what they had done" (Revelation 20:12, ESV). Here, the full weight of our earthly accountability to divine truth will be manifest.

In the Christian faith, truth and accountability are not merely parallel tracks but intertwined realities that deeply influence one another. Truth informs and shapes accountability, while accountability gives life and substance to truth. Together, they form a comprehensive framework for understanding God, relating to Him, and living in a manner worthy of His calling. Therefore, as believers committed to the totality of Scripture, we must continually seek to deepen our grasp of divine truth while holding ourselves and others accountable to it. This dynamic interplay between truth and accountability serves as a powerful catalyst for spiritual growth, community building, and ultimately, the glory of God.

The Consequences of Ignoring Truth

The concept of truth holds an eminent position in Christian theology and practice. Regarded as the revealed will of God primarily manifested in the person of Jesus Christ and the Scriptures, truth functions as the bedrock on which Christian ethics, doctrine, and conduct are built. However, with the gravity of truth comes the weighty matter of the repercussions that follow when truth is ignored or rejected. The Bible offers ample warning and examples of what happens when individuals or communities disregard divine truth. This discussion aims to explore these consequences in a scriptural context, recognizing the sobering implications for today's believers.

A Defiance of God's Nature

Ignoring truth is not merely a matter of personal choice; it is a defiance of the very nature of God, who is the embodiment of truth (John 14:6). When David pleaded for divine intervention in his life, he appealed to God's truthful nature, saying, "Lead me in your truth and teach me" (Psalm 25:5, ESV). Defying the truth amounts to defying God Himself, with spiritual repercussions that can be severe (Romans 1:18-25).

Spiritual Blindness

One of the most alarming consequences of ignoring truth is spiritual blindness. Jesus mentioned this when He spoke about the religious leaders of His day, who were blind guides leading the blind (Matthew 15:14). Ignoring God's truth dulls spiritual sensitivity, resulting in an inability to discern right from wrong, holy from profane.

The Danger of Deception

A disregard for truth opens the door for deception. Paul warns that in the last days, people will "not endure sound teaching, but having itching ears they will accumulate for themselves teachers to suit their own passions" (2 Timothy 4:3, ESV). The rejection of truth sets up a breeding ground for false doctrines and misleading ideologies that can shipwreck faith.

Decline of Moral Integrity

Ignoring divine truth invariably leads to the decay of moral and ethical standards. Paul's letter to the Romans outlines the downward spiral of those who "exchanged the truth about God for a lie" (Romans 1:25, ESV). This abdication of truth results in all manner of ungodliness and wickedness, pulling the individual and, eventually, the community, further away from God's standards.

Relational Strain

Truth is relational at its core. Ignoring truth creates a barrier in our relationship with God and with others. In a marital context, for example, the violation of truth through dishonesty can cause irreparable damage. The same holds true in our relationship with God. Unconfessed sin and the rejection of divine truth disrupt fellowship and can lead to spiritual barrenness (Isaiah 59:2).

Jeopardizing Salvation

While salvation is by grace through faith, it is a grave mistake to assume that ignoring truth has no eternal consequences. Hebrews 10:26-27 warns that if we go on sinning deliberately after receiving the knowledge of the truth, there no longer remains a sacrifice for sins, but a fearful expectation of judgment. While salvation is a gift, it does not negate the call to live a life of obedience and truth.

Divine Discipline

Scripture makes it clear that God disciplines those He loves (Hebrews 12:6). When believers persist in ignoring truth, they place themselves in a position to be disciplined by God. This disciplinary action aims to correct and restore, yet it can be a painful process and should serve as a caution to heed truth earnestly.

The Impact on Witness

Ignoring truth also tarnishes our witness to the world. Jesus said, "You are the light of the world" (Matthew 5:14, ESV). This light dims when truth is compromised, causing the world to question the efficacy and integrity of the Christian message. In a time when the truth of the Gospel is critically needed, adherence to truth must be non-negotiable for the Christian community.

Loss of Spiritual Power and Authority

Truth carries with it spiritual power and authority. When ignored or substituted with human wisdom, the believer experiences a loss of spiritual potency. Instead of operating in the "power of God," one runs the risk of becoming like the Pharisees, who were well-versed in the Scriptures but devoid of spiritual power due to their hypocrisy and manipulation of truth (Matthew 23).

Ignoring truth carries severe consequences that affect every facet of life—spiritual, relational, moral, and even eternal. It sets individuals and communities on a path that diverges from God's intended plan, leading to a myriad of adverse outcomes. The warnings are laid out clearly in Scripture and serve as a grave reminder of the crucial role that truth plays in the Christian life. As custodians of this truth, we have a sacred responsibility to honor, uphold, and live by it. Ignoring truth is not merely risky; it is a perilous choice with profound implications. Therefore, in our journey of faith, let us heed the Apostle Paul's advice to "speak the truth in love" (Ephesians 4:15, ESV) and to "take every thought captive to obey Christ" (2 Corinthians 10:5, ESV). It is only through a steadfast commitment to truth that we can hope to live lives that are pleasing to God, effective in witness, and fruitful in eternal outcomes.

JAMES 5:19 If Any Among You Strays from the Truth and One Turns Him Back

The Risk of Straying from Truth

The closing verse of the Epistle of James is striking in its gravity and immediacy. James 5:19 states, "My brothers, if anyone among you wanders from the truth and someone brings him back" (ESV). The implication is unambiguous: even within the community of believers, there exists a real and pressing danger of deviating from the truth. The focus of this essay is to delve into the inherent risks associated with straying from the truth and the Scriptural directives for mitigating these hazards.

The Nature of Truth in James

In James, "truth" is closely linked to a right understanding of God's will and living it out in practice. This is an objective truth, not subject to human interpretation but revealed through God's Word. It manifests in actions that correspond with faith, aligning with the greater biblical teaching that faith without works is dead (James 2:17).

The Susceptibility to Stray

Straying from the truth is not presented as a remote possibility but a probable risk. It can happen subtly, often through gradual negligence or indifference toward Scriptural teaching. This is consistent with other biblical admonitions about the dangers of drifting away from the faith (Hebrews 2:1).

Intellectual Deviation

Straying from truth is not merely a behavioral issue but often begins with intellectual deviation. Misinterpretations of Scripture, embracing heretical teachings, or the influence of worldly philosophies can precipitate a departure from truth. Paul addresses this in Colossians 2:8, cautioning against being taken captive by "philosophy and empty deceit" (ESV).

Ethical Compromise

In other cases, straying from the truth manifests in ethical and moral compromises. What may begin as a seemingly inconsequential decision can lead to a life that is profoundly misaligned with God's will. Peter highlights this when he discusses those who have escaped the defilements of the world and then become entangled and overcome again (2 Peter 2:20).

Erosion of Integrity

When one strays from the truth, there is a consequent erosion of personal integrity. This compromises the individual's witness and effectiveness in the ministry, hindering the proclamation of the Gospel. Paul reminds Timothy to be a "worker...rightly handling the word of truth" (2 Timothy 2:15, ESV), highlighting the relationship between integrity and adherence to truth.

Spiritual Consequences

The spiritual ramifications are perhaps the most alarming. Straying from the truth can lead to a hardened heart, less sensitive to the conviction of the Holy Spirit. The danger is that this can culminate in apostasy, an irreversible state of rebellion against God (Hebrews 6:4-6).

Community Impact

The risk of straying from the truth is not only a personal matter but also affects the community of believers. A single individual's deviation can lead to divisions and factions within the church. This is evidenced by Paul's letters to the Corinthians, where he corrects numerous doctrinal and ethical errors that were causing disunity (1 Corinthians 1:10-13).

The Role of Correction

James 5:19 implies a community responsibility to correct the one who strays. This is not merely an individual endeavor but a collective one, underscoring the importance of community in safeguarding the truth. This aligns with Galatians 6:1, where believers are instructed to restore those caught in transgressions.

Eternally Significant

The consequences of straying are not just temporally significant; they bear eternal weight. James 5:20 states, "let him know that whoever brings back a sinner from his wandering will save his soul from death and will cover a multitude of sins" (ESV). Here the stakes are made clear: the straying individual risks not only temporal but eternal loss, emphasizing the gravity of staying aligned with truth.

Preventive Measures

Scripture offers preventive measures to mitigate the risk of straying. These include diligent study of the Word, communal accountability, consistent prayer, and the cultivation of spiritual discernment. The objective is to build a life so grounded in truth that the risk of straying is minimized.

The possibility of straying from truth is real, significant, and fraught with severe spiritual, ethical, and eternal consequences. It serves as a warning to individuals and communities alike to be vigilant in maintaining a steadfast commitment to God's truth as revealed in Scripture. It also underscores the importance of community in both preventing and correcting deviations. Truth is not a negotiable or mutable concept but an objective standard revealed by God. To stray from it is to risk walking a path that leads away from God's will, jeopardizing both temporal effectiveness and eternal destiny. Therefore, we should heed the words of James and be diligent in our efforts to both adhere to and uphold the truth of God's Word.

The Community's Role in Restoration

The role of the community—commonly understood as the congregation of believers—in spiritual restoration is a theme richly interwoven throughout the fabric of the New Testament. Given the focus on individualistic spirituality in contemporary Christianity, there is a pressing need to re-examine and underscore the collective responsibility of the community in the restoration of a fallen member. This essay will navigate through pertinent Scriptures to distill the theological foundations and practical implications of this essential community role.

The Concept of Community in the New Testament

In the New Testament, the Greek term "ekklesia" is often translated as "church," but it more accurately refers to a gathering or assembly of people. This body is not merely an institutional entity but a living organism connected by faith in Jesus Christ. When one member is in spiritual disarray, it is not just an individual problem but a communal concern.

The Weight of Collective Responsibility

Paul's epistles often articulate the interdependence among believers. One such key text is Galatians 6:1, which states: "Brothers, if anyone is caught in any transgression, you who are spiritual should restore him in a spirit of gentleness" (ESV). The term "restore" here carries with it the idea of setting something back to its original condition. The restoration of a transgressing member, therefore, is not an option but an obligation borne by the spiritually mature within the community.

The Mechanics of Restoration

Restoration is not a one-size-fits-all process; it involves a nuanced approach taking into account the specific needs of the individual. James 5:19-20 suggests that the goal is to turn the sinner back from his erroneous ways, thus saving his soul from death. This is a process that requires discernment, love, and wisdom, and not simply dogmatic enforcement of community standards.

The Necessity of Gentleness and Humility

In correcting the one who has strayed, Paul emphasizes gentleness as a crucial attitude (Galatians 6:1). This is not a sign of compromise but a recognition of one's own susceptibility to sin. It is with a humble acknowledgment of our own weaknesses that we can approach a fallen brother or sister, seeking to restore them.

Collective Accountability

Restoration also involves communal examination. Paul's advice to the Corinthians in 1 Corinthians 5:1-5 is instructive. He exhorts the church to remove the immoral member, not as a punitive measure, but to bring about repentance and eventual restoration. The community, in this sense, is responsible for creating an environment conducive to spiritual growth and repentance.

Safeguarding against Apostasy

The writer of Hebrews provides another lens to view communal responsibility. In Hebrews 3:12-13, the author warns against the "deceitfulness of sin" and recommends mutual exhortation to prevent a hardened heart. In other words, the community serves as a safeguard against the risks of spiritual apostasy that often start subtly.

The Role of Leadership

While restoration is a collective responsibility, the role of spiritual leadership is undeniably important. Elders and pastors are often entrusted with the pastoral care necessary for restoration. They are called to exercise this authority not as lords over the congregation but as shepherds guiding the flock (1 Peter 5:2-3).

Implications for Church Discipline

Church discipline, often perceived negatively, is actually a means for restoration. Matthew 18:15-20 outlines a process that culminates in treating the unrepentant individual "as a Gentile and a tax collector" (ESV). While this may seem harsh, the purpose remains restorative. The hope is that the seriousness of excommunication will lead to repentance and reintegration into the community.

A Picture of Divine Restoration

The ultimate goal of community-driven restoration is to reflect the redemptive work of Christ. Through His death and resurrection, Jesus restored fallen humanity's relationship with God, providing a model for us to emulate in our interpersonal relations.

Eternal Relevance

The stakes in the restoration process are high. The failure to restore a straying member can have eternal consequences. Conversely, a successful restoration results not just in temporal well-being but in eternal salvation (James 5:20).

The community's role in the restoration of its members is not merely a suggestion but a Scriptural imperative. The process may be complex and fraught with challenges, but it is a necessary endeavor commanded by Scripture and modeled by Christ. It serves both as a preventive measure against spiritual decline and as a curative approach for those who have fallen. Far from being a mere institutional function, restoration is at the heart of what it means to be a community of believers, bound together by the truth of the Gospel and the hope of eternal life. Therefore, it behooves us to take this responsibility seriously, executing it with grace, humility, and an unwavering commitment to Scriptural truth.

The Importance of Vigilance

The concept of vigilance is deeply embedded in Scripture and represents an essential aspect of the Christian walk. Vigilance—often synonymous with watchfulness, alertness, and preparedness—is neither optional nor arbitrary but rooted in God's character and explicitly directed towards sustaining our faith amid spiritual warfare, false teachings, and even apathy. This essay will explore the Biblical imperative for vigilance, its different facets, and its importance in the life of the believer.

Vigilance as a Divine Imperative

The clarion call to vigilance rings through both the Old and New Testaments. We find it in the wisdom literature: "Keep your heart with all vigilance, for from it flow the springs of life" (Proverbs 4:23, ESV). In the New Testament, Jesus exhorts His disciples in the Garden of Gethsemane: "Watch and pray that you may not enter into temptation" (Matthew 26:41, ESV). The urgency of the command signifies its fundamental role in spiritual vitality.

Vigilance in Spiritual Warfare

Scripture is unequivocal about the reality of spiritual warfare. Paul explicitly tells the Ephesian church to "Put on the whole armor of God, that you may be able to stand against the schemes of the devil" (Ephesians 6:11, ESV). Notably, the Apostle Peter, who himself learned the hard way about the perils of spiritual complacency, counsels, "Be sober-minded; be watchful. Your adversary the devil prowls around like a roaring lion, seeking someone to devour" (1 Peter 5:8, ESV). Vigilance is not about paranoia but an acknowledgment of the spiritual hostilities that surround us and our dependence on God's strength.

Vigilance against False Teachings

As we proceed towards the eschatological future, the Bible warns us of the increasing prevalence of false doctrines and teachings. In Acts 20:28-31, Paul warns the Ephesian elders to be vigilant for themselves and the flock, stating that "savage wolves will come in among you." Vigilance is vital in discerning these distortions and safeguarding the purity of the Gospel.

Vigilance and Moral Integrity

Paul tells Timothy to "flee youthful passions and pursue righteousness, faith, love, and peace, along with those who call on the Lord from a pure heart" (2 Timothy 2:22, ESV). Fleeing and pursuing are active verbs requiring continuous, deliberate actions. The vigilance in maintaining moral integrity is not just an individual endeavor but a communal one, implying accountability and collective righteousness.

The Perils of Apathy

It is possible for vigilance to wane due to spiritual apathy, which Scripture sternly warns against. The church at Laodicea was rebuked for being "neither cold nor hot" (Revelation 3:16, ESV), while the writer of Hebrews cautions against neglecting such a great salvation (Hebrews 2:3). Spiritual lethargy is antithetical to vigilance and poses a serious risk to the integrity of our faith.

Vigilance and the Eschatological Hope

Scripture often ties vigilance to the return of Christ. The parable of the ten virgins (Matthew 25:1-13) and Christ's admonition to "stay awake, for you do not know on what day your Lord is coming" (Matthew 24:42, ESV) emphasize the eternal importance of being spiritually alert. The end goal of vigilance is not merely temporal well-being but an eternal communion with God.

The Role of Prayer

Vigilance is closely linked to prayer. As Jesus directed His disciples, "Watch and pray." Prayer not only attunes our spirit to God's will but also reinforces our spiritual alertness. It becomes a means through which we cultivate an attitude of vigilance.

Accountability in Vigilance

The importance of community in maintaining vigilance can't be understated. "Let us consider how to stir up one another to love and good works" (Hebrews 10:24, ESV). The community serves as a system of checks and balances, ensuring that individual members are upheld in their efforts to be vigilant.

The Promise of Divine Assistance

Though the task may seem daunting, the believer is not left alone in his vigilance. Divine help is available. "But the Helper, the Holy Spirit, whom the Father will send in my name, he will teach you all things and bring to your remembrance all that I have said to you" (John 14:26, ESV).

Vigilance is not a sporadic or occasional requirement but a continuous obligation. It is a comprehensive term that incorporates spiritual warfare, discernment, moral integrity, and a host of other elements crucial to the faith. The call to vigilance is both a divine imperative and an indispensable human responsibility, with eternal implications. We are invited to live this out in community, sustained by the grace of God, and driven by the hope of eternal life in Christ.

The Reward of Reclaiming a Straying Soul

The ministry of reclaiming souls that have strayed from the faith is a theme that runs deeply through Scripture. From the Old Testament prophets calling Israel back to faithfulness to Jesus' parables about lost sheep, the Bible consistently portrays God's heart for the erring and the role believers play in their restoration. This essay aims to explore the theological foundations, ethical implications, and eternal rewards of engaging in the ministry of reclaiming straying souls.

The Theological Foundations for Restoration

To fully grasp the reward of reclaiming a straying soul, one must first understand the theological backdrop. According to the Bible, human beings are created in the image of God (Genesis 1:26-27) and are souls in essence (Genesis 2:7). Sin causes estrangement from God, but the work of Christ on the cross allows for reconciliation (Romans 5:10). This grand narrative of redemption sets the stage for individual restoration efforts, mirroring on a smaller scale the cosmic restoration initiated by God Himself.

Jesus as the Model Restorer

Our primary model for the restoration of straying souls is Jesus. The parable of the lost sheep in Luke 15:3-7 reveals the extent to which the Good Shepherd will go to find and restore one lost sheep. The joy that follows the restoration is not just an individual celebration but a communal and heavenly one, emphasizing the eternal significance of the act.

Ethical Implications

Restoring a straying soul isn't merely an optional act of charity; it's an ethical mandate grounded in love and accountability. James 5:19-20 makes this point strikingly clear: "My brothers, if anyone among you wanders from the truth and someone brings him back, let him know that whoever brings back a sinner from his wandering will save his soul from death and will cover a multitude of sins" (ESV). This implies a level of mutual responsibility within the Christian community to be vigilant and proactive in restoration efforts.

Spiritual Warfare and Restoration

Restoring a straying soul is an act that is deeply embedded in spiritual warfare. The Apostle Peter warns, "Be sober-minded; be watchful. Your adversary the devil prowls around like a roaring lion, seeking someone to devour" (1 Peter 5:8, ESV). The act of reclaiming a straying soul involves spiritual discernment and often a battle against demonic influences that seek to ensnare the individual further.

The Eternal Rewards

The Bible outlines eternal rewards for faithfulness in various forms of ministry, and the task of restoring a straying soul is no exception. The apostle Paul speaks of the believer's works being tested by fire, and what is of eternal value will receive a reward (1 Corinthians 3:12-15). There's a profound eternal joy in knowing that one has been an instrument in saving a soul from eternal destruction and facilitating its pathway to eternal life.

Reclaiming as an Act of Worship

The act of reclaiming a straying soul should not be viewed merely as a human endeavor but as a form of worship that aligns us with God's redemptive agenda. Just as Jesus came "to seek and to save the lost" (Luke 19:10, ESV), so do we reflect the heart of God when we participate in the restoration of erring individuals.

Practical Aspects of Reclaiming

The process of reclaiming a straying soul involves several practical steps, including confrontation, counsel, prayer, and often, communal intervention. The manner in which this is done is crucial; Galatians 6:1 advises that it should be a gentle restoration, done in a spirit of humility. The end goal is not merely the cessation of sinful behavior but the full spiritual rehabilitation of the individual.

Emotional and Psychological Dimensions

Restoration often involves an intense emotional and psychological journey for both the one restoring and the one being restored. Genuine love, empathy, patience, and resilience are needed to navigate through the complex maze of human emotions and rationalizations that often accompany a season of spiritual drifting.

The Role of Repentance

It's crucial to note that the act of reclaiming is not a unilateral effort that ignores the will of the straying individual. True restoration requires repentance, a turning away from sin and a return to God, which the erring person must willingly undertake.

The reward of reclaiming a straying soul is multifaceted, encompassing eternal, ethical, and relational dimensions. Rooted in the character of God and modeled by Jesus, the task of restoration is a grave responsibility that holds immense eternal significance. It aligns us with the heart of God, enriches our community, fortifies us in spiritual warfare, and offers the indescribable joy of seeing a life redirected toward its eternal purpose. Thus, reclaiming a straying soul is not merely a Christian obligation but a divine privilege with eternal dividends.

1 PETER 1:22 By Your Obedience to the Truth

The Call to Obedience

The theme of obedience to the truth is a cornerstone in Christian doctrine, with roots extending from the Mosaic Law to the teachings of Christ and the Apostles. This paper will focus on understanding the call to obedience as expressed in 1 Peter 1:22, which states: "Having purified your souls by your obedience to the truth for a sincere brotherly love, love one another earnestly from a pure heart" (ESV). The passage provides a rich theological insight into how obedience to the truth serves as a transformative agent in the life of a believer, leading to a life characterized by sincere love for one's brethren.

Contextual Analysis

To understand the full impact of this verse, one must first look at its context. The Apostle Peter was writing to Christians scattered due to persecution, exhorting them to stand firm in their faith. The entire chapter of 1 Peter 1 is a blend of affirmations about the believers' secure status because of Christ's redemption and their ensuing responsibilities. The notion of obedience is not an isolated command but part of a broader ethical framework rooted in the salvific work of Christ.

The Concept of Obedience

The term "obedience" as used in this verse bears considerable weight. It is derived from the Greek word "hupakoē," which signifies attentive listening and submission. It presupposes a standard to which one conforms, and in the Christian context, that standard is none other than the truth of God's Word. Obedience in the biblical sense, then, is not mere external compliance but involves a transformation of the will and inner disposition.

The Truth as the Basis for Obedience

The term "truth" in this verse refers to the revealed will of God, as encapsulated in the Holy Scriptures. The word "truth" (Greek: "alētheia") signifies what is real, reliable, and in accordance with what is. The biblical notion of truth is not abstract but relational—it reveals the very character and plans of God. To obey the truth is to align oneself with God's purposes, to live in accordance with His character, and to be guided by His Spirit-inspired Word.

Purification of the Soul

The verse explicitly links obedience to the truth with the purification of the soul. The term "soul" here aligns with the Hebrew concept of "nephesh," which refers to the entire self—emotions, will, and intellect. In this context, "purification" implies an ethical cleansing, an internal renovation that makes a person fit for communion with God and fellow humans. This purification is not a human achievement but a consequence of obeying the revealed truth of God.

Sincere Brotherly Love

One of the direct outcomes of this purification is "sincere brotherly love." The text uses the term "philadelphia," which signifies the love that should exist between members of a spiritual family. This is not a superficial, sentimental love but one that is earnest, arising from a "pure heart." It implies actions, sacrifices, and a commitment to the well-being of others. This kind of love is only possible when the soul has been purified by obedience to God's truth.

Obedience as a Continuous Call

In the Christian life, obedience is not a one-time event but a continuous, lifelong process. The Apostle Paul wrote that the believer should be "transformed by the renewal of your mind" (Romans 12:2, ESV), signaling an ongoing transformation. Likewise, Peter's exhortation implies a sustained effort in obeying the truth and loving one another, underpinned by constant engagement with the Word of God.

The Reciprocal Relationship Between Obedience and Love

It is worth noting that obedience to the truth not only leads to sincere brotherly love but that such love can also reinforce obedience. John, another apostle, makes this clear in his writings when he asserts that love for God is made manifest in our obedience to His commands (1 John 5:3). This suggests a virtuous cycle where obedience engenders love, and love fuels further obedience.

The Eschatological Implications

The obedient life does not go unrewarded. Scripture is clear that there will be an assessment of each believer's works (2 Corinthians 5:10), and those works that withstand the divine evaluation will be rewarded. Thus, the call to obedience carries both temporal and eternal implications.

1 Peter 1:22 serves as a compelling text that dives deep into the transformative power of obedience to the truth. Obedience is shown to purify the soul, set the stage for authentic Christian community through brotherly love, and align the believer with the eternal purposes of God. The verse seamlessly links theology with ethics, doctrine with practice, and individual piety with communal responsibilities. Therefore, the call to obedience in this passage is not a burdensome command but a liberating principle that unshackles the believer from sin, fosters genuine love, and aligns one's will with the divine, fulfilling the ultimate purpose for which humans were created—to glorify God and enjoy Him forever.

Truth as the Foundation for Christian Living

The centrality of truth in the Christian life is a theme that traverses the length and breadth of Scripture. The Apostle John unequivocally declared that God is "spirit, and those who worship him must worship in spirit and truth" (John 4:24, ESV). This underscores the indispensable role of truth as the foundation for Christian living. This essay aims to explore the theological and ethical dimensions of truth, its implications for the Christian community, and the personal responsibilities it entails for individual believers.

Defining Biblical Truth

In biblical terms, "truth" (Greek: "alētheia") encompasses what is real, reliable, and in accordance with what is. The word is not an abstract concept but is deeply relational and covenantal, rooted in the character of God Himself. It is revealed through the life, teachings, and work of Jesus Christ, who declared Himself to be "the way, and the truth, and the life" (John 14:6, ESV).

The Source of Truth: God's Word

The divine source of all truth is God's Word. Jesus prayed for His disciples saying, "Sanctify them in the truth; your word is truth" (John 17:17, ESV). This underlines the importance of the Scriptures as the infallible repository of divine truth. Every instruction, command, and doctrinal formulation must be tested against the standard of Scripture.

The Importance of Truth in Salvation

Truth is not merely a philosophical concept but has salvific implications. The Apostle Paul noted that the gospel is "the word of truth, the gospel of your salvation" (Ephesians 1:13, ESV). Believing the truth about Christ's life, death, and resurrection is essential for salvation. It is through the message of truth that the Holy Spirit convicts the world of sin, righteousness, and judgment (John 16:8).

The Role of Truth in Sanctification

Sanctification, the process of becoming more like Christ, is closely tied to truth. Paul writes that believers are to be "sanctified by the truth" (John 17:17). This implies that living a holy life is conditioned upon the continuous absorption and application of biblical truth. The Word of God is the "sword of the Spirit" (Ephesians 6:17, ESV), effective for rebuking, correcting, and training in righteousness (2 Timothy 3:16).

Truth and Christian Ethics

Ethical living is intrinsically linked to truth. Falsehood and deceit are strongly condemned throughout Scripture, while integrity and honesty are extolled (Ephesians 4:25; Colossians 3:9). Moreover, Jesus identified truth as the axis on which the two greatest commandments—loving God and loving neighbor—turn. He said, "You shall love the Lord your God with all your heart and with all your soul and with all your mind. This is the great and first commandment. And a second is like it: You shall love your neighbor as yourself" (Matthew 22:37-39, ESV). Love, in its truest form, is an expression of truth.

The Community of Truth: The Church

The Church is described as "the pillar and foundation of the truth" (1 Timothy 3:15, ESV). This implies that the community of believers has the solemn duty to uphold and disseminate the truth. Church practices, whether corporate worship, discipleship, or community engagement, should be grounded in truth. Any compromise on this essential foundation can lead to heresy and disunity.

Truth and the Last Days

The New Testament repeatedly warns against the proliferation of false teachings and apostasy in the last days (2 Timothy 4:3-4; 2 Peter 2:1). The safeguard against such deception is a firm grounding in the truth of God's Word. Moreover, adhering to the truth has eschatological implications; it prepares believers for the judgment to come, where they will give an account of their lives (2 Corinthians 5:10).

Personal Responsibility and Accountability

Christians are individually responsible for their interaction with truth. The Bereans were commended for examining the Scriptures daily to verify Paul's teachings (Acts 17:11). Furthermore, believers are exhorted to "speak the truth in love"

(Ephesians 4:15, ESV) and to "walk in truth" (3 John 1:4). This suggests that truth is not just a doctrinal position but a way of life that requires continuous commitment and vigilance.

Challenges in Upholding Truth

Modern society often espouses a relativistic view of truth, where it is subject to individual interpretation. This is fundamentally at odds with the biblical understanding of truth as absolute and unchanging. Christians must be discerning and equipped to counter such ideologies by "rightly handling the word of truth" (2 Timothy 2:15, ESV).

Truth is not merely an accessory to the Christian faith; it is its very foundation. It emanates from God, finds its ultimate expression in Jesus Christ, and is recorded in the Scriptures. Truth plays a crucial role in salvation, sanctification, and ethical living. As members of the Church, Christians have a collective and individual responsibility to uphold and propagate this truth, particularly in a culture increasingly indifferent or even hostile to it. Therefore, truth indeed forms the bedrock upon which the edifice of Christian living is built.

The Link Between Obedience and Love

The nexus between obedience and love is a recurring motif in Christian thought and theology, deeply rooted in the biblical narrative. Although these two concepts might seem distinct, Scripture binds them together in a theological tapestry that informs our understanding of God, our relationship with Him, and our interactions with others. This essay aims to delve into the intricate link between obedience and love as portrayed in Scripture, exploring its theological implications, ethical mandates, and practical applications for the believer.

The Source of Love and Obedience: God's Character

Understanding the relationship between obedience and love begins with an exploration of God's character. Scripture states unequivocally that God is love (1 John 4:8, ESV). Jehovah's love is manifest in His actions toward humanity, most notably in the sending of His Son, Jesus Christ, for the world's salvation (John 3:16). Moreover, God's moral law reflects His character and His love. When we obey God, we are aligning ourselves with His character and participating in His love.

Love and the Law

In the Old Testament, the giving of the Law on Mount Sinai can be viewed as an act of love. This provided Israel with ethical, social, and religious guidelines that, if followed, would set them apart as God's chosen people. Moses encouraged Israel to "love Jehovah your God and keep His charge, His statutes, His rules, and His commandments always" (Deuteronomy 11:1, ESV). The Law was not an arbitrary set of rules but a pathway to enjoying a relationship based on love and trust with God.

Love in the New Covenant

The New Testament presents love and obedience in a renewed light, particularly through the life and teachings of Jesus Christ. Jesus said, "If you love me, you will keep my commandments" (John 14:15, ESV). Here, love and obedience are intrinsically connected: love motivates obedience, and obedience validates love. This isn't legalism but rather a relational dynamic that stems from the love of God poured into our hearts (Romans 5:5).

The Greatest Commandment: A Summation of Law and Love

Jesus identified the greatest commandments as loving God with all one's heart, soul, and mind and loving one's neighbor as oneself (Matthew 22:36-40). All the Law and the Prophets, Jesus stated, hang on these two commandments. It is fascinating to note that the call to love is couched in the language of commandment, thereby linking love and obedience inseparably. In fulfilling these commandments, we exhibit the highest form of both love and obedience.

Love as an Indicator of Discipleship

Jesus further stated that love would be the defining characteristic of His disciples. "By this all people will know that you are my disciples, if you have love for one another" (John 13:35, ESV). This love is not abstract but is demonstrated through obedient actions such as self-sacrifice, service, and the bearing of one another's burdens (Galatians 6:2). It is our obedience to the command to love that marks us as genuine followers of Christ.

Ethical Implications: The Moral Law as a Guide to Love

Ethically, love provides the motivation for obedience to God's moral laws. The Apostle Paul asserts that love fulfills the law, summarizing commandments like "You shall not commit adultery; You shall not murder; You shall not steal" under the banner of "love your neighbor as yourself" (Romans 13:8-10, ESV). Thus, obedience to God's commandments is a practical outworking of love, not a means to earn God's favor.

Obedience and Love in Trials

Scripture makes it clear that trials and difficulties are inevitable in the Christian life (James 1:2-4). It is in these times that our love and obedience are tested the most.

In suffering, we echo Christ's obedience, rooted in love for the Father, even when obedience led Him to the cross (Philippians 2:5-8).

The Community Aspect: Obedience and Love in the Church

In the body of Christ, love and obedience find a communal expression. The Apostle John emphasizes that one cannot love God and hate his brother (1 John 4:20). Similarly, communal obedience reinforces collective identity as the people of God, exemplifying the love of Christ in interactions both within and outside the community.

Challenges and Pitfalls

Despite the clear biblical teaching, challenges abound in living a life marked by love and obedience. Legalism, the notion that obedience earns divine favor, is a perennial pitfall. On the other hand, antinomianism, which eschews obedience in the name of a distorted concept of love, is equally dangerous. Both extremes misrepresent the biblical relationship between love and obedience.

The relationship between obedience and love is not one of tension but of beautiful harmony. Rooted in God's character and culminating in the person and work of Jesus Christ, this intricate connection provides the framework for Christian ethics, discipleship, and community. In an increasingly relativistic culture, this biblically rooted understanding of love and obedience serves as a timeless anchor, guiding the believer toward a life that is pleasing to God and beneficial to others.

The Outcomes of Truthful Obedience

The topic of truthful obedience is a cornerstone in Christian theology and practice, offering us a panoramic view of the significance of aligning our will with the will of God as revealed in Scripture. Obedience to truth is not simply an ethical obligation but a dynamic force with far-reaching consequences for both the individual and the collective body of believers. This essay aims to explore the outcomes that result from truthful obedience in the context of Christian life, church community, and personal transformation.

The Theological Framework: Divine Revelation and Human Response

At the heart of truthful obedience is the notion of divine revelation. Scripture serves as God's revelation of truth, the benchmark for what we believe and how we behave. "All Scripture is breathed out by God and profitable for teaching, for reproof, for correction, and for training in righteousness" (2 Timothy 3:16, ESV). In turn, the human response to this revelation is obedience, which functions as a barometer of our relationship with God.

Personal Transformation: The Fruit of the Spirit

One of the most evident outcomes of truthful obedience is personal transformation. Paul describes this transformation as the "fruit of the Spirit" which includes love, joy, peace, patience, kindness, goodness, faithfulness, gentleness, and self-control (Galatians 5:22-23, ESV). These virtues are not the result of human effort but are born out of obedience to the Spirit's leading through the Word of God. It is, therefore, no surprise that James calls believers to be "doers of the Word, and not hearers only" (James 1:22, ESV).

Sanctification: Growing in Christlikeness

Truthful obedience plays a critical role in the process of sanctification, which refers to the lifelong journey of becoming more like Christ. Jesus prayed, "Sanctify them in the truth; your word is truth" (John 17:17, ESV). When we obey the truth of Scripture, we are aligning ourselves with God's purposes and, in doing so, experiencing ongoing sanctification.

Relational Benefits: Intimacy with God

Obedience to God's truth strengthens our relationship with Him. Jesus said, "Whoever has my commandments and keeps them, he it is who loves me. And he who loves me will be loved by my Father, and I will love him and manifest myself to him" (John 14:21, ESV). This mutual intimacy is one of the profound outcomes of truthful obedience and represents the pinnacle of Christian experience.

The Ecclesiological Implications: Unity and Witness

In the context of the church, obedience to the truth serves to foster unity and effective witness. The Apostle Paul urged the Ephesian church to "walk in a manner worthy of the calling to which you have been called, with all humility and gentleness, with patience, bearing with one another in love, eager to maintain the unity of the Spirit in the bond of peace" (Ephesians 4:1-3, ESV). A church that is obedient to the truth of Scripture stands as a united body, drawing others into the saving knowledge of Jesus Christ.

Ethical Integrity: Living Righteously in a Fallen World

Truthful obedience also bears fruit in the form of ethical integrity. Peter exhorts believers to "be holy in all your conduct" because God is holy (1 Peter 1:15-16, ESV).

A life of obedience stands as a testament to the transformative power of the gospel, and it sets a moral standard that serves as a light in a fallen world.

Eternal Rewards: Crowns and Commendation

The New Testament hints at the eternal rewards awaiting those who faithfully obey God's truth. Paul speaks of "crowns of righteousness" for those who have fought the good fight and have remained faithful (2 Timothy 4:7-8). Though our ultimate motivation should be love for God rather than the expectation of reward, the prospect of eternal commendation remains an encouraging outcome of truthful obedience.

Challenges and Dangers: Legalism and Self-Righteousness

While considering the outcomes of obedience, it is crucial to be aware of the pitfalls like legalism and self-righteousness. Obedience should be born out of love for God, not as a means to earn salvation or favor. For "by grace you have been saved through faith. And this is not your own doing; it is the gift of God, not a result of works" (Ephesians 2:8-9, ESV).

Truthful obedience to the Word of God yields manifold outcomes that are transformative both at an individual and communal level. From personal sanctification to corporate unity and effective witness, the impact of living in alignment with divine truth cannot be overstated. In an age characterized by moral relativism and spiritual apathy, the call to truthful obedience serves as a clarion call for the church to stand firm on the Word of God, inviting believers into a life of profound purpose, transformation, and eternal significance.

1 JOHN 2:21 No Lie Is of the Truth

The Incompatibility of Lies and Truth

The epistle of 1 John serves as an invaluable resource for understanding the nature of truth in the context of Christian belief and conduct. Among the salient passages is 1 John 2:21, which states, "I write to you, not because you do not know the truth, but because you know it, and because no lie is of the truth" (ESV). This seemingly straightforward statement is packed with theological and ethical implications. It highlights the incompatibility between lies and truth, thus illuminating a foundational principle for Christian living. This essay aims to expound on the text, considering its relevance and application in the contemporary Christian context.

Contextual Understanding: The Johannine Perspective

The epistle was written in a context where false teachings and heresies were beginning to infiltrate the church. Gnosticism, which denied the incarnation of Christ among other things, was particularly prevalent. John's statement is therefore not merely a truism but a potent counter to erroneous teachings that were corrupting the foundational truths of Christianity. It reminds the readers that truth and falsehood cannot coexist in harmony within the framework of Christian orthodoxy.

The Theological Imperative: Divinely Revealed Truth

One of the underpinnings of the Christian faith is the belief in divinely revealed truth, chiefly manifested through the Scripture and the person of Jesus Christ. The Apostle Paul writes that "all Scripture is breathed out by God and profitable for teaching, for reproof, for correction, and for training in righteousness" (2 Timothy 3:16, ESV). Jesus Himself is described as the "Word" that became flesh, full of grace and truth (John 1:14). This divine source of truth serves as the ultimate standard against which all claims, teachings, and practices are to be measured.

The Ethical Implications: Lies as a Violation of Truth

When John states that "no lie is of the truth," he is also delving into ethical territory. Lies are not just incorrect statements; they are violations of the truth and therefore offensive to the nature of a God who is defined by truth. The Ten Commandments include the admonition not to bear false witness, underlining the gravity with which God views the act of lying (Exodus 20:16).

Personal Integrity: Living in the Truth

The incompatibility between lies and truth has significant implications for personal Christian integrity. John is calling for a lifestyle that reflects the truth of the gospel, a life that is transparent before God and men. This integrity is not only personally transforming but serves as a witness to others. Peter urges believers to "keep your conduct among the Gentiles honorable, so that when they speak against you as evildoers, they may see your good deeds and glorify God" (1 Peter 2:12, ESV).

The Ecclesial Dimension: Truth in the Church Community

The concept extends beyond individual ethics to the collective ethos of the church. The New Testament frequently warns against false teachers and prophets who introduce heresies and thereby distort the truth (2 Peter 2:1; Galatians 1:6-9). A vigilant church that holds to the apostolic teachings acts as a bulwark against such distortions and serves as a beacon of truth in a world mired in falsehoods.

The Dangers of Syncretism and Compromise

In an age that celebrates pluralism and relativism, the church faces the danger of diluting the truth through syncretism and compromise. When John declares that "no lie is of the truth," he is providing a prophetic warning against such tendencies. To mix lies with truth is not only to compromise the gospel but to partake in something fundamentally antithetical to the nature of God.

Consequences of Ignoring Truth

Neglecting or altering the truth has serious ramifications. Scripture warns that there will be "itching ears" that turn away from listening to the truth and wander off into myths (2 Timothy 4:3-4). Such departure from the truth can lead to spiritual stagnation, doctrinal error, and even apostasy.

The Hope in Adherence to Truth

On a more hopeful note, adherence to truth is equated with walking in the light and having fellowship with God (1 John 1:6-7). The Psalmist declares that God's word is a lamp to guide our feet and a light for our path (Psalm 119:105), indicating that walking in truth has the outcome of divine guidance and fellowship.

1 John 2:21 stands as a sentinel, reminding us of the uncompromising nature of divine truth. In a world that often blurs the lines between fact and fiction, right and wrong, the apostle John calls us back to the steadfast standard of God's revealed truth. The incompatibility between lies and truth serves as a cornerstone principle that shapes

our theology, our ethics, and our community life as followers of Christ. It reminds us that fidelity to the truth is not an option but an obligation, laden with profound implications for our personal lives, our churches, and indeed, our eternal destinies.

Discerning Spiritual Deception

Spiritual deception is an age-old issue that continues to plague the church. The very word "deception" implies an infringement upon truth, which is paramount for the Christian faith. Given that truth is integral to a proper understanding of God and His plans for humanity, any form of deception is not only dangerous but potentially devastating. Discernment, therefore, becomes a critical skill in navigating the Christian life, safeguarding both the individual believer and the collective church body from going astray. In this essay, we will explore the biblical guidelines for discerning spiritual deception.

The Reality of Spiritual Deception: Scriptural Testimonies

The Bible does not mince words about the existence of spiritual deception. Jesus himself warns, "Beware of false prophets, who come to you in sheep's clothing but inwardly are ravenous wolves" (Matthew 7:15, ESV). The Apostle Paul further alerts the Ephesian elders that "savage wolves will come in among you, not sparing the flock; and from among your own selves will arise men speaking twisted things, to draw away the disciples after them" (Acts 20:29-30, ESV).

The Source of Deception: Satan, the Father of Lies

Understanding the source of deception aids in discernment. The Bible identifies Satan as the father of lies (John 8:44). His modus operandi from the very beginning—tempting Eve in the Garden of Eden—has been to sow doubt, twist Scripture, and propagate falsehoods. He often employs agents—false teachers and false prophets—to disseminate these deceptions.

The Vulnerability to Deception: The Human Condition

Why are humans susceptible to spiritual deception? The Bible offers a sobering diagnosis: the sinful nature. Jeremiah states, "The heart is deceitful above all things, and desperately sick; who can understand it?" (Jeremiah 17:9, ESV). This inherent moral corruption makes individuals more prone to embracing falsehoods, especially those that align with their desires and preconceptions.

The Protective Measure: Sound Doctrine

Sound doctrine serves as the first line of defense against spiritual deception. Paul instructs Timothy to "preach the word; be ready in season and out of season; reprove, rebuke, and exhort, with complete patience and teaching" (2 Timothy 4:2, ESV). A well-grounded theological understanding, based on the objective Historical-Grammatical method of interpretation, equips believers to recognize and reject false teachings.

Discernment through the Spirit-Inspired Word of God

While the Holy Spirit does not indwell believers in a mystical sense, His guidance comes through the Spirit-inspired Word of God. By studying the Scriptures diligently, Christians equip themselves with the divine wisdom necessary for discernment. The psalmist writes, "Your word is a lamp to my feet and a light to my path" (Psalm 119:105, ESV).

The Accountability of Spiritual Leaders

Leaders within the church bear a weighty responsibility for safeguarding the flock against spiritual deception. James warns, "Not many of you should become teachers, my brothers, for you know that we who teach will be judged with greater strictness" (James 3:1, ESV). This underscores the importance of integrity and doctrinal accuracy among those in leadership positions.

Testing the Spirits: Objective Criteria

John advises believers to "test the spirits to see whether they are from God, for many false prophets have gone out into the world" (1 John 4:1, ESV). But what are the criteria for such testing? A teacher's adherence to core doctrinal truths—such as the deity and humanity of Christ, the inspiration of Scripture, and the necessity of grace for salvation—often serves as a reliable yardstick.

Discernment in Community: The Church as a Pillar of Truth

Individual discernment should be corroborated within the context of a community of believers. Paul describes the church as "a pillar and buttress of the truth" (1 Timothy 3:15, ESV). The collective wisdom and diverse gifts within a church body can often provide a more nuanced and comprehensive discernment.

Consequences of Ignoring Spiritual Deception

Ignoring or underestimating the problem of spiritual deception can lead to devastating outcomes—heretical beliefs, fractured communities, and ultimately, eternal separation from God. The issue is not merely academic but one of eternal significance.

The threat of spiritual deception is real and should be taken seriously. The Bible provides a robust framework for discerning truth from falsehood, rooted in the objective standards of God's Word. Through diligent study of the Scriptures, a commitment to sound doctrine, and mutual accountability within the church, believers can guard themselves against the insidious dangers of spiritual deception. This is not just a matter of intellectual integrity but of spiritual survival. Let us, therefore, heed the scriptural admonitions and cultivate discernment as a vital Christian discipline.

The Importance of Abiding in Truth

The concept of "truth" is central to Christianity. Jesus declares Himself to be "the way, and the truth, and the life" (John 14:6, ESV). Indeed, the Bible as the Spirit-inspired Word of God is the ultimate repository of divine truth, and Christians are called to live in a manner congruent with its teachings. However, the act of abiding in truth is not merely an intellectual endeavor. It has profound implications for one's spiritual health, community, and eternal destiny. This essay will explore the importance of abiding in truth from a biblical perspective, emphasizing its foundational role in Christian living.

Truth as the Touchstone of Authentic Faith

Truth is not a relative or subjective idea within the Christian framework. The Bible presents it as an objective standard rooted in the very nature of God Himself. Jehovah is described as a God "who cannot lie" (Titus 1:2, ESV). As believers, embracing and abiding in truth become the hallmarks of an authentic relationship with Him. Jesus asserts, "If you abide in my word, you are truly my disciples, and you will know the truth, and the truth will set you free" (John 8:31-32, ESV). Here, truth is both liberating and defining—it frees us from sin's bondage and marks us as genuine followers of Christ.

Truth as a Means of Sanctification

Sanctification, the process of becoming more Christ-like, is intimately linked with truth. Jesus prays for His followers, saying, "Sanctify them in the truth; your word is truth" (John 17:17, ESV). The divine standard of truth serves as the moral and spiritual compass guiding us on the path of sanctification. Without a steadfast commitment to biblical truth, one risks succumbing to moral compromise and spiritual stagnation.

Truth and the Integrity of the Church

The church is called to be the "pillar and buttress of the truth" (1 Timothy 3:15, ESV). Abiding in truth is not just an individual mandate but a corporate one. When a community of believers is committed to biblical truth, it creates an environment conducive to spiritual growth, mutual accountability, and effective witness. Conversely, deviation from truth can lead to doctrinal error, disunity, and the discrediting of the Gospel message.

Truth as a Guard Against Deception

In a world awash with conflicting ideologies and spiritual counterfeits, the ability to discern truth from falsehood becomes critical. The Apostle Paul warns against being "tossed to and fro by the waves and carried about by every wind of doctrine, by human cunning, by craftiness in deceitful schemes" (Ephesians 4:14, ESV). Abiding in truth acts as a bulwark against such deception, enabling believers to recognize and resist erroneous teachings.

The Objective Standard: The Spirit-Inspired Word of God

While the Holy Spirit does not indwell believers in some mystical fashion, His guidance is accessible through the Word of God. A systematic and prayerful study of Scripture, applying the Historical-Grammatical method of interpretation, equips us with the intellectual and spiritual tools to discern and abide in truth. The Apostle Paul aptly advises Timothy to be a workman "rightly handling the word of truth" (2 Timothy 2:15, ESV).

The Role of Spiritual Leadership in Upholding Truth

Leaders in the Christian community bear a unique responsibility to uphold and disseminate truth. James warns that teachers will be judged more strictly (James 3:1, ESV). They are not only accountable for their own walk in truth but are also stewards of the spiritual well-being of those under their care. Their teaching must adhere to sound doctrine, and their lives must exemplify the biblical standards of integrity and holiness.

Eternal Implications of Abiding in Truth

Finally, the imperative to abide in truth has eternal implications. The Bible makes it clear that the rejection of truth leads to spiritual and eternal peril. Paul states that the wrath of God is revealed against "unrighteous men who suppress the truth" (Romans 1:18, ESV). Furthermore, salvation itself is received "in accordance with the truth of the Gospel" (Galatians 2:5, ESV). Hence, the choice to abide in truth is ultimately a choice that impacts one's eternal destiny.

Truth, as revealed in the Spirit-inspired Scriptures, serves as both the foundation and the guiding principle for a life that is pleasing to God. From defining authentic faith to facilitating the sanctification process, from preserving the integrity of the church to safeguarding against spiritual deception, the importance of abiding in truth is manifold. The Bible offers a robust framework that underscores the centrality of truth, not as an abstract concept but as an objective standard that governs every aspect of Christian living. To disregard or compromise on this bedrock is to risk spiritual waywardness and eternal loss. Thus, the call to abide in truth is not optional but essential, not just for the individual believer but for the Christian community as a whole. It is a call to a life of enduring commitment, steadfast obedience, and eternal hope.

The Role of Integrity in Faith

Integrity, often defined as the quality of being honest and having strong moral principles, is a value highly esteemed in both secular and religious circles. However, within the Christian context, integrity takes on even deeper significance. It is not merely a sociocultural norm but a spiritual mandate, rooted in the very character of God and His revelation in Scripture. This essay aims to examine the role of integrity in faith from a conservative Christian perspective, relying on the Spirit-inspired Word of God as the ultimate standard of truth.

Integrity as a Reflection of God's Character

God is the epitome of integrity. He is "faithful and just" (1 John 1:9, ESV), "a God of faithfulness and without iniquity, just and upright is he" (Deuteronomy 32:4, ESV). As Christians, we are called to be imitators of God (Ephesians 5:1), which includes mirroring His integrity in our lives. To claim faith in Jehovah while living incongruently with His character represents a profound spiritual dissonance.

Integrity in Personal Piety

The relationship between integrity and faith begins on a personal level, within the recesses of the individual's heart. King David's prayer, "Create in me a clean heart, O

God, and renew a right spirit within me" (Psalm 51:10, ESV), underscores the integral relationship between personal piety and integrity. A sincere faith naturally leads to a life of integrity, devoid of hypocrisy. The Apostle James reminds us that faith without works is dead (James 2:17), meaning a proclaimed faith that does not manifest in a life of integrity is questionable at best.

Integrity in Doctrinal Matters

Sound doctrine is non-negotiable for the believer committed to living with integrity. The Apostle Paul urges Timothy to keep a "good conscience, so that when you are slandered those who revile your good behavior in Christ may be put to shame" (1 Peter 3:16, ESV). Diligent study and correct interpretation of Scripture are essential for ensuring that the doctrines we espouse align with God's truth. Paul also instructs Timothy to "rightly handle the word of truth" (2 Timothy 2:15, ESV), emphasizing the integrity required in the realms of teaching and doctrine.

Integrity in Relationships and Community Life

Integrity is not limited to individual character and doctrinal fidelity; it extends to how one interacts with others both within and outside the community of faith. The Bible admonishes us to "speak the truth in love" (Ephesians 4:15, ESV), and to engage in relationships characterized by honesty, trustworthiness, and mutual edification. The Apostle Paul's exhortation to "Let love be genuine" (Romans 12:9, ESV) captures the essence of integrity in Christian relationships.

Integrity in Witnessing and Service

Our interactions with the world also need to be marked by integrity. We are ambassadors for Christ (2 Corinthians 5:20), and our life of integrity either validates or undermines our testimony. Scripture emphasizes the importance of conducting oneself with integrity in the world (Philippians 2:15), such that even those who oppose you may "see your good deeds and glorify God" (1 Peter 2:12, ESV).

Integrity and Spiritual Accountability

Living a life of integrity opens the believer up to the mechanism of accountability, both to God and to the spiritual community. This is not merely a burdensome obligation but an expression of the New Testament model of fellowship. Accountability fosters spiritual growth and ensures that one's practice of faith remains consistent with the tenets of Scripture.

Integrity and the Final Judgment

The question of integrity transcends the bounds of earthly existence and has eschatological implications. Jesus Himself declared, "For what will it profit a man if he gains the whole world and forfeits his soul? Or what shall a man give in return for his soul?" (Matthew 16:26, ESV). At the final judgment, each one will give an account of their lives, and it is the integrity of one's faith that will stand the test (2 Corinthians 5:10).

The role of integrity in faith is multifaceted, extending from personal piety to doctrinal fidelity, and from relational ethics to public witness. This is not an optional add-on but an essential component, intricately woven into the fabric of authentic Christian living. Given its foundational importance, it is crucial to maintain a life of integrity as an expression of our commitment to Jehovah and His revealed truth in Scripture. Anything less than this would be incongruent with the Gospel message and the example set by Jesus Christ. To walk in integrity is to walk in alignment with God's will, thus fulfilling the purpose for which we have been called: to glorify God and enjoy Him forever. In doing so, we can have confidence that our faith is not just a nominal affiliation but a life-transforming reality.

2 JOHN 1:1-2 All Who Know the Truth Because of the Truth that Remains in Us

The Community Bound by Truth

The Second Epistle of John, though brief, carries a message of monumental importance, underscoring the critical role of truth in the life of the Christian community. Verses 1 and 2 of the first chapter poignantly lay the foundation: "The elder to the elect lady and her children, whom I love in truth, and not only I but also all who know the truth, because of the truth that abides in us and will be with us forever" (2 John 1:1-2, ESV). This exposition aims to unpack the richness embedded in these verses, demonstrating that truth is not merely a concept or doctrine but the very lifeblood that sustains and unites the Body of Christ.

The Elder and the Elect Lady

The letter is penned by "the elder," likely the Apostle John, and is directed toward "the elect lady and her children." Although some propose that this is a metaphor for a local church and its members, the message remains the same: The truth of the Gospel forms the backbone of the Christian relationship, whether that relationship is between individual believers or entire congregations.

Love Rooted in Truth

John emphasizes that his love for the recipients is rooted in truth: "whom I love in truth." In a world where "love" is often detached from objective standards and devolves into mere sentimentality or emotionalism, John's statement is a powerful reminder. Love, devoid of truth, risks becoming a shallow or even destructive force. In contrast, love anchored in truth is stable, genuine, and aligned with God's own character.

The Universal Appeal of Truth

Importantly, John extends the circle of this truth-based love beyond himself: "and not only I but also all who know the truth." Truth is not the private possession of a few enlightened individuals or a single community; it is the shared heritage of all who are in Christ. By virtue of their allegiance to the truth, Christians worldwide are knit into a single, unified body.

The Abiding Nature of Truth

John adds another layer of significance by saying this love and knowledge are "because of the truth that abides in us." Truth is not a fleeting or changing principle; it remains constant and is meant to abide or remain in believers. This permanence of truth reinforces the long-term commitment believers are to have with one another. It's not a transient, conditional association but a lasting, indestructible bond, held together by the abiding truth of the Gospel.

The Eternal Perspective

John concludes with an eschatological note: the truth "will be with us forever." While truth remains unchanging, it is not static. It is dynamic, living, and eternal, continually breathing life into the community of faith. The truth we uphold today has an eternal aspect, pointing us toward our ultimate hope and calling in Christ. This perspective should bring sobriety and seriousness to our commitment to the truth, as it is not just for this present life but for the life to come.

The Community Bound by Truth

For John, the community of faith is essentially a community bound by truth. It is not held together by cultural ties, emotional affinity, or social compatibility, as significant as these might be in other contexts. The essence of Christian community is the shared commitment to the eternal, abiding truth as revealed in Scripture. This truth governs every relationship, every interaction, and every endeavor of the community of faith. It serves as the ultimate litmus test for the authenticity and vitality of our love for one another.

Accountability to the Truth

Being bound by truth involves more than mere agreement; it entails a mutual accountability to live in accordance with that truth. This notion of accountability is in line with other passages where Scripture explicitly holds leaders and members within the community responsible for upholding the truth (1 Timothy 4:16; Titus 1:9).

The Counter-Cultural Implication

In a culture that often promotes relativism and celebrates individual autonomy, a community bound by objective, eternal truth is profoundly counter-cultural. The church, as such a community, stands as a living testimony to a world lost in subjectivism and moral chaos. It declares that truth is not a construct but a divine revelation, not an option but an obligation, and not a preference but a precept.

The opening verses of 2 John serve as a compact but potent affirmation of the integral role of truth in the Christian community. In a world swaying to the whims of relativism and subjective notions of love, the epistle calls believers back to the unchanging, abiding, and eternal truth of God. Our commitment to this truth is not merely an intellectual exercise but a life-transforming reality that binds us together in genuine love and mutual accountability. Anything less would be a departure from our calling and a betrayal of the community that God Himself has established through His eternal truth. Therefore, may we be a people "bound by truth," living out our faith with the integrity, commitment, and love that such a calling demands.

The Enduring Nature of Divine Truth

The notion of "truth" in contemporary society is increasingly subjected to relativistic interpretations, implying that what may be true for one person is not necessarily true for another. Against the backdrop of this relativism, the Bible stands as an immovable pillar, offering divine truths that are not subject to human fickleness. One of the most striking features of Biblical revelation is the enduring nature of divine truth. This article aims to explore this significant characteristic, underscoring how it impacts the life of the believer and the integrity of the Christian faith.

The Timeless Essence of Truth

Divine truth is not circumscribed by the shifting sands of time. It transcends cultural nuances, social trends, and ideological movements. Isaiah 40:8 says, "The grass withers, the flower fades, but the word of our God will stand forever" (ESV). In a world of constant change, the truth of God provides a stable, unchanging foundation. Divine truth is not subject to revisions, alterations, or updates; it is eternally settled. As the Psalmist declares, "Forever, O Jehovah, your word is firmly fixed in the heavens" (Psalm 119:89, ESV).

Immutable and Inerrant

The truth that comes from God is both immutable and inerrant. It does not change because God Himself is unchanging (Malachi 3:6; Hebrews 13:8). Moreover, it is without error because it originates from a God who is perfect and who cannot lie (Numbers 23:19; Titus 1:2). These aspects reinforce the enduring nature of divine truth. They attest to its reliability and trustworthiness, forming the basis upon which faith and practice can securely rest.

Universality of Divine Truth

The enduring nature of divine truth is not confined to a particular geographic location or demographic. It is universal, applying equally to all people, in all places, and at all times. The Apostle Paul makes this clear in Romans 2:14-15, discussing how the moral law is written on the hearts of even those who do not have the written law. The truth of God is so pervasive and enduring that it transcends human divisions and speaks to the conscience of every person.

Sufficient for Every Generation

Each generation faces its unique challenges and questions, but the enduring nature of divine truth means that it is sufficient for the needs of every generation. Whether it was the early church grappling with the issue of Gentile inclusion (Acts 15) or Christians today dealing with ethical questions surrounding technology, the truth of God provides adequate guidance and wisdom. Second Timothy 3:16-17 declares that "All Scripture is breathed out by God and profitable for teaching, for reproof, for correction, and for training in righteousness, that the man of God may be complete, equipped for every good work" (ESV).

The Consummation of Truth in Christ

In the New Testament, we find that the enduring nature of divine truth reaches its zenith in the person and work of Jesus Christ. Jesus Himself declared, "I am the way, and the truth, and the life" (John 14:6, ESV). He is the living embodiment of truth, and in Him, all the promises and revelations of God find their "Yes" and "Amen" (2 Corinthians 1:20). The Gospel of Christ is not a fleeting message relevant only for a particular time; it is the eternal truth offering salvation to all who believe (Romans 1:16).

The Implications for the Believer

The enduring nature of divine truth has profound implications for the Christian life. Firstly, it offers an objective standard by which ethical and moral decisions can be made. Secondly, it provides a source of unchanging hope and comfort in times of distress and uncertainty. Thirdly, it demands allegiance and obedience, calling believers to anchor their lives in truth rather than the shifting values of the world (Romans 12:1-2).

The Dangers of Ignoring the Enduring Nature of Truth

Rejecting the enduring nature of divine truth results in spiritual instability and deception. It opens the door for false doctrines and deviant practices, undermining the integrity of the faith (Ephesians 4:14; 2 Timothy 4:3-4). When the enduring truth of God is compromised, the community of believers is weakened, and its witness to the world is tarnished.

In a world that continues to relativize truth, the enduring nature of divine truth stands as a beacon calling humanity back to its Creator. The truth revealed in the Scriptures and personified in Christ does not change; it is immutable, inerrant, universal, and eternally relevant. It is the solid ground upon which believers can stand and the unchanging standard by which they must live. Ignoring this enduring truth is perilous, but embracing it leads to life eternal, making the believer "wise for salvation through faith in Christ Jesus" (2 Timothy 3:15, ESV). Therefore, in an age of fleeting certainties and transient allegiances, may the church be a bulwark of enduring divine truth, to the glory of God and the edification of souls.

The Reciprocal Relationship Between Knowing and Living the Truth

Within Christian theology, one of the most essential and yet often overlooked concepts is the symbiotic relationship between knowing the truth and living it out. This connection goes far beyond cognitive assent; it is the conduit through which faith in Christ manifests in daily life. This article will explore the nuances of this reciprocal relationship, emphasizing its roots in Scripture and its vital role in sustaining a flourishing Christian life.

The Scriptural Basis for Knowing the Truth

The Bible consistently presents the concept of truth as something to be known and internalized. Jesus asserts, "You will know the truth, and the truth will set you free" (John 8:32, ESV). The Apostle Paul urges Timothy to "rightly handle the word of truth" (2 Timothy 2:15, ESV). The term 'know' here isn't a mere intellectual understanding but implies a deep, internal realization that influences one's actions. Such knowledge forms the foundation upon which the Christian life is built.

The Imperative to Live Out the Truth

While knowing the truth is crucial, the Bible is clear that this knowledge must lead to action. James warns against being mere hearers of the word and not doers, equating such behavior to self-deception (James 1:22-25). John echoes this sentiment, stating,

"Little children, let us not love in word or talk but in deed and in truth" (1 John 3:18, ESV). For John, the measure of truth isn't merely what we confess but also what we practice.

The Interconnectedness of Knowing and Living the Truth

The correlation between knowing the truth and living it out is not linear but reciprocal. One informs and enriches the other in a continuous loop. When you know the truth, it should compel you to live according to it. Conversely, living out the truth enriches your understanding of it. It's akin to a marriage where love and respect are mutually reinforcing.

Implications for Personal Piety

The link between knowing and living the truth has profound implications for personal piety. Knowing the truth ought to fuel a life of prayer, devotion, and obedience to God's commands. On the other hand, living a life of holiness and righteousness reinforces and clarifies our understanding of the truth. For example, it is one thing to know that God is faithful; it is another to experience His faithfulness by living in a way that depends on Him.

Implications for Social Ethics

This reciprocal relationship also extends to how we interact with society at large. Knowing the Biblical principles for justice, mercy, and love should lead to a life committed to these virtues. Conversely, our engagement with the world informs and refines our understanding of these principles. This is not a call to conform to the world but to be transformed by the renewing of our minds, "so that by testing you may discern what is the will of God, what is good and acceptable and perfect" (Romans 12:2, ESV).

Implications for Evangelism and Discipleship

Understanding the integral connection between knowing and living the truth is pivotal for both evangelism and discipleship. A Gospel proclaimed without a life lived in congruence with it is severely hampered. Paul epitomizes this when he notes that his life aims to magnify Christ so that his message is not discredited (Philippians 1:20-21).

Guarding Against Disparities

The Christian community must be vigilant to ensure that the gap between knowing and living the truth does not widen. In the words of the Apostle Paul, we must "examine yourselves, to see whether you are in the faith. Test yourselves" (2 Corinthians 13:5, ESV). This self-examination is not a solitary endeavor but should occur within the context of a local church where accountability structures are in place.

The Role of the Holy Scriptures

The Scriptures play a critical role in facilitating this reciprocal relationship. As the inspired Word of God, they are the "lamp to our feet and a light to our path" (Psalm 119:105, ESV). Regular engagement with the Scriptures sharpens both our understanding and application of the truth.

The Danger of Imbalance

An imbalance between knowing the truth and living it out can lead to two extremes. On the one hand, mere intellectual knowledge without application can result in spiritual pride and dead orthodoxy. On the other hand, attempting to live out what one does not fully understand can lead to legalism or moralism.

In summary, the reciprocal relationship between knowing and living the truth is neither optional nor supplementary; it is foundational to Christian life and thought. This symbiotic relationship ensures that faith is not relegated to mere intellectual assent but is lived out in tangible, transformative ways. Moreover, it serves as a safeguard against the perils of hypocrisy and dead orthodoxy. For the believer earnestly striving to follow Christ, this interconnectedness between knowing and living the truth is not just a doctrine to be affirmed but a life to be lived to the glory of God.

The Unified Testimony of Truthful Lives

The idea of a unified testimony of truthful lives is pivotal in the context of Christian ethics, doctrine, and community. This concept elucidates how the integrity and actions of individual believers contribute to a collective witness for the Gospel of Jesus Christ. In a world where the church is often criticized for hypocrisy and moral failure, a cohesive and consistent demonstration of truthful living is a compelling apologetic that substantiates the claims of Christianity. This essay will examine the Biblical foundation, implications, and outworking of this idea, affirming the necessity of both individual and communal fidelity to the truth.

Biblical Foundation

The New Testament is replete with examples and exhortations that encourage believers to live out their faith authentically. Jesus Christ Himself set the standard, living a life entirely consistent with His teachings (1 Peter 2:21-22). Paul urged the Ephesian church to "walk in a manner worthy of the calling to which you have been called" (Ephesians 4:1, ESV). He also commended the Thessalonians for becoming "an example to all the believers" due to their work of faith and labor of love (1 Thessalonians 1:7-8, ESV).

Individual Responsibility to Truth

In the framework of Christianity, the obligation to truth starts at an individual level. James makes it clear that a person who claims to have faith but does not have works is a practitioner of a dead faith (James 2:17, ESV). Paul, in his letters, often emphasizes that the believer's body is a temple of the Holy Spirit, and thus should be used for righteousness (1 Corinthians 6:19-20, ESV). The goal is to "shine as lights in the world" (Philippians 2:15, ESV), which each believer must aim to do in their spheres of influence.

Communal Responsibility to Truth

Christianity, however, is not an individualistic faith. Believers are parts of a larger Body—the Church (1 Corinthians 12:12-27, ESV). This makes the collective witness of a Christian community equally important. In His high priestly prayer, Jesus prayed for His disciples "that they may become perfectly one, so that the world may know that you sent me" (John 17:23, ESV). The unified testimony of a community living truthfully is a powerful witness to the world and provides a validating proof for the Gospel message.

The Symbiosis of Individual and Communal Responsibility

The relationship between individual and communal truthfulness is symbiotic. When believers in a community adhere to Biblical truth in their personal lives, it strengthens the community's witness. Conversely, a strong, truth-abiding community also helps to encourage and uphold the individual in their pursuit of truthful living. This cycle of mutual strengthening creates a "city set on a hill" that cannot be hidden (Matthew 5:14, ESV).

Practical Outworking

The practical outworking of a unified testimony involves personal disciplines like Bible study, prayer, and ethical living, coupled with communal practices like corporate worship, accountability, and collective social engagement. It is in the synthesis of these that a compelling testimony takes form. Spiritual leaders bear a particular responsibility in teaching sound doctrine and modeling integrity (Titus 2:7-8, ESV).

Contemporary Relevance

In an era of relative truth and moral decline, the unified testimony of truthful lives is like a beacon in the darkness. When individual Christians and the collective Church uphold truth, it serves as a countercultural statement that demands attention. Such unified witness can open doors for evangelism, social justice, and transformative engagement with culture.

The Dangers of Disunity and Hypocrisy

When there is disunity or inconsistency between proclamation and practice, it damages both the individual and collective testimonies. As Jesus warned, a house divided against itself cannot stand (Mark 3:25, ESV). Inconsistencies and failures need to be addressed and corrected through Biblical church discipline and individual repentance.

The Role of Truth in Persecution and Suffering

In a world that often rejects absolute truth, adherence to the principles of Scripture might invite persecution or marginalization. Yet, it is precisely in these circumstances that a unified testimony of truthful lives becomes a compelling witness for the Gospel (1 Peter 3:15-17, ESV).

The idea of a unified testimony of truthful lives is not a secondary or optional aspect of Christian living; it is a Biblically mandated, essential component. It bears significance for personal ethics, communal conduct, and the Church's engagement with the world. By adhering to the truth in both individual and collective contexts, believers reflect the character of God, validate the Gospel message, and fulfill their role as salt and light in a decaying and darkened world. This responsibility is sobering but also empowering, as it offers an opportunity to participate in God's redemptive work on earth. Therefore, every effort should be made to strengthen this unified testimony, as it is crucial for the credibility and effectiveness of the Christian witness.

Bibliography

Anders, M. (1999). *Holman New Testament Commentary: vol. 8, Galatians-Colossians*. Nashville, TN: Broadman & Holman Publishers.

Anders, M. (2005). *Holman Old Testament Commentary - Proverbs*. Nashville: B&H Publishing.

Anders, M., & Lawson, S. (2004). *Holman Old Testament Commentary - Psalms: 11*. Grand Rapids: B&H Publishing.

Andrews, E. D. (2016). *INTERPRETING THE BIBLE: Introduction to Biblical Hermeneutics.* Cambridge, OH: Christian Publishing House.

Andrews, E. D. (2022). *THE LETTER OF JAMES: An Apologetic and Background Exposition of the Holy Scriptures (CPH New Testament Commentary).* Cambridge, Ohio: Christian Publishing House.

Andrews, E. D. (2023). *BIBLICAL EXEGESIS: Biblical Criticism on Trial.* Cambridge, OH: Christian Publishing House.

Andrews, E. D. (2023). *THE BOOK OF PROVERBS Chapters 1-15: CPH Old Testament Commentary: Volume 17.* Cambridge, OH: Christian Publishing House.

Andrews, E. D. (2023). *THE BOOK OF PROVERBS Chapters 16-23: CPH Old Testament Commentary: Volume 18.* Cambridge, OH: Christian Publishing House.

Andrews, E. D. (2023). *THE OLD TESTAMENT: Commentary, Background, & Bible Difficulties (Introduction to the Old Testament).* Cambridge, OH: Christian Publishing House.

Boa, K., & Kruidenier, W. (2000). *Holman New Testament Commentary: Romans.* Nashville: Broadman & Holman.

Borchert, G. L. (2001). *The New American Commentary: John 1-11*. Nashville, TN: Broadman & Holman Publishers.

Borchert, G. L. (2002). *The New American Commentary vol. 25B, John 12–21.* Nashville: Broadman & Holman Publishers.

Brand, C., Draper, C., & Archie, E. (2003). *Holman Illustrated Bible Dictionary: Revised, Updated and Expanded.* Nashville, TN: Holman.

Bromiley, G. W. (1986). *The International Standard Bible Encyclopedia (Vol. 1-4).* Grand Rapids, MI: William B. Eerdmans Publishing Co.

Bromiley, G. W., & Friedrich, G. (1964-). *Theological Dictionary of the New Testament, ed. Gerhard Kittel, vol. 4.* Grand Rapids, MI: Eerdmans.

Bruce, F. F. (1990). *The New International Commentary on the New Testament: The Epistle to the Hebrews (Revised).* Grand Rapids, MI: William B. Eermans Publishing Company.

Carson, D. A. (1991). *The Gospel according to John, The Pillar New Testament Commentary.* Leicester, England; Grand Rapids, MI: Inter-Varsity Press; W.B. Eerdmans, 1991.

Elwell, W. A. (2001). *Evangelical Dictionary of Theology (Second Edition).* Grand Rapids: Baker Academic.

Elwell, W. A., & Beitzel, B. J. (1988). *Baker Encyclopedia of the Bible.* Grand Rapids, MI: Baker Book House.

Gangel, K. O. (2000). *Holman New Testament Commentary, vol. 4, John.* Nashville, TN: Broadman & Holman Publishers.

Guthrie, G. H. (1998). *The NIV Application Commentary: Hebrews.* Grand Rapids, MI: Zondervan.

Kistemaker, S. J. (1984). *Baker New Testament Commentary: Hebrews.* Grand Rapids: Baker Books.

Kistemaker, S. J., & Hendriksen, W. (1953-2001). *New Testament Commentary: Exposition of Paul's Epistle to the Romans.* Grand Rapids, MI : Baker Book House .

Lea, T. D. (1999). *Holman New Testament Commentary: Hebrews, James.* Nashville, TN: Broadman & Holman Publishers.

Longman III, T. (2015). *Proverbs (Baker Commentary on the Old Testament Wisdom and Psalms).* Grand Rapids, MI: Baker Academic.

Marshall, T. F. (2023). *THE NEW TESTAMENT: Its Background, Setting & Content.* Cambridge, Ohio: Christian Publishing House.

Marshall, T. F., & Andrews, E. D. (2022). *PAUL'S LETTER TO THE PHILIPPIANS: An Apologetic and Background Exposition of the Holy Scriptures.* Cambridge, Ohio: Christian publishing House.

Moo, D. J. (1996). *The Epistle to the Romans (New International Commentary on the New Testament).* Grand Rapids, MI: William B. Eerdmans Publishing Company.

Pratt Jr, R. L. (2000). *Holman New Testament Commentary: I & II Corinthians, vol. 7.* Nashville: Broadman & Holman Publishers.

Vine, W. E., Unger, M. F., & White Jr., W. (1996). *Vine's Complete Expository Dictionary of Old and New Testament Words.* Nashville, TN: T. Nelson.

Walls, D., & Anders, M. (1996). *Holman New Testament Commentary: I & II Peter, I, II & III John, Jude.* Nashville: Broadman & Holman Publishers.

Wood, D. R. (1996). *New Bible Dictionary (Third Edition)*. Downers Grove: InterVarsity Press.

www.ingramcontent.com/pod-product-compliance
Lightning Source LLC
LaVergne TN
LVHW061332060426
835512LV00013B/2610